GREY MATTER
Dialogues

GREY MATTER
Dialogues

*A Journey on Economics and History
of Science and Technology*

JOSEPH ANTONY PULIKKOTTIL

PARTRIDGE

ISBN: Hardcover   978-1-5437-0019-0
               Softcover   978-1-5437-0018-3
               eBook   978-1-5437-0017-6

To order additional copies of this book, contact
Partridge India
000 800 10062 62
orders.india@partridgepublishing.com

www.partridgepublishing.com/india

CONTENTS

PREFACE

Are you feeling overwhelmed, stressed or disorientated in your daily life? It is not surprising.

It's because we are currently living in one of the most dynamic periods in the history of human civilization. The human race had experienced such cultural and economic shock during the time of Renaissance, which lasted from 1450 to 1550. It was a period of great discoveries and accomplishments, ranging from the development of printing press to new forms of arts that culminated in the masterpieces of Michelangelo and Leonardo Da Vinci. The world economy and social strata that we see today had its origins during this time. As we saw in Renaissance, the modern era is transforming through global information exchange enabled by the internet and new media. Despite the innovations made during this period by the likes of astronomer Nicolaus Copernicus, theologian Martin Luther, and explorer Christopher Columbus, the Renaissance was also a time of great destruction and suffering.

Diseases such as smallpox spread across oceans, practically exterminating the Aztecs, Incas and other Native Americans. Just like the Renaissance of the fifteenth century, we are currently in the technology Renaissance. The New Renaissance could be said to have started in 1990 with the fall of the Berlin Wall and the end of the Cold War. The beginning of the commercial internet service and entry of China into the world economy marked the arrival of the new renaissance. However, just like the Renaissance of past centuries, this progress came with a hefty bill. This unprecedented development took a catastrophic toll on the environment. Was this development worth it? Did it increase human convenience?

Where could we possibly be heading with these technologies? What technologies could find a way to the future?

I have tried to focus my humble efforts on understanding how such technologies would benefit mankind mostly from an economic sense. If we look back at our world a mere 25 years ago, it will be practically unrecognizable from the one that is existing now. Politics, the economy, and society have all dramatically transformed. For instance, centuries ago, the printing press revolutionized the communication that was limited to a single lifetime. When the German entrepreneur Johann Gutenberg invented movable type printing press he transformed the mankind that had to rely solely on face-to-face conversations and handwritten manuscripts for communication. Similarly, the internet has transformed the way people interact today. Since 1988, when the first intercontinental fiber-optic cables were installed, the number of users connected through this infrastructure has grown more than seven-fold. In 2000 it was 400 million; in 2005, it was one billion, and by 2017 it had reached 3.75 billion, i.e, half the world population.

The internet age marked easily the fastest mass adoption of a technology in the whole of human history, and one that radically connected all of the humanity. On the global health and wealth, the humanity is at its highest level ever, even for the most disadvantaged populations on earth. Life expectancy has risen by almost two decades since 1960, climbing from 52 to 71 years. To put that in perspective, the last 20-year improvement in this metric took 1,000 years to achieve, not 50. As a result, a baby born today in practically any country can expect to live longer than at any previous point in that country's history.

The progress that we see today is the result of interconnected economies. The expansion of trade and the jobs it has raised the incomes of poor people. Competition has increased, which has, in turn, lowered the prices of goods and services while boosting their quality. The incredible accomplishments realized during the first Renaissance and the new Renaissance makes it seem like a magnificent cornucopia of progress. On the flip side, there were clear signs that the progress attained during this period had disparate outcomes. While average welfare rose during much of the period, the wealth gap between rich and poor grew dramatically. Exact data from the first Renaissance is a bit patchy, but all the information that's available points to a rise in income inequality alongside the expansion of manufacturing and trade. To give a perspective, between 1480 and 1562, a nanny's wages did not increase at all, yet the cost of her daily necessities rose by 150 percent. The similar shift is being seen with the advent of the new technology. Unsurprisingly, a polarity between rich and poor is also central to our current Renaissance and the supreme power of technology is going to increase the divide of the rich and poor.

In addition, the rich will be having much more resources to become richer and to ensure that poor do not become rich and the poor will still be deprived of such privileges making them continue in the same social strata. While average global welfare is rising, the extremes have grown even more distant. In 2010, the 388 richest people in the world controlled more wealth than the poorest 50 percent of the population. By 2015, this number dropped dramatically as just 62 people controlled more wealth than the bottom half. Meanwhile, the bottom 50 percent of society – some 3.6 billion people globally – subsist on an average of just a few dollars per day.

The technology has made our world so interconnected that the side-effects of positive or negative phenomena are visible across continents. In fact, the interconnectivity of the modern world means that when something happens far away, it's likely to rapidly become a problem at home. Just consider the 2008 financial crisis, which began in the United States but swiftly became a global issue. Or take cyber attacks: these data crimes can be committed anywhere in the world and prey on anybody, anywhere. Through this book, I have tried to give perspectives on the future based on the history of the scientific evolution and how these technologies could change the world as we see today. I have tried to give a few perspectives on the impact of these technologies in our everyday life and the practical transformations that we could see.

And now who should read this book? This is definitely for people who are interested to know where technology is headed. This book is equally relevant for the someone who is aspiring to understand the future of our world. Anyone who is interested to choose the areas to study for the future could find this book handy and inspiring. At the minimum, I am sure that everyone is curious to know how did we humans evolve and what are we doing globally on technology and the effects of such developments on society and the planet. Finally, the unintended beneficiaries would include the investors, entrepreneurs, and students who have interests on future technologies and science that could touch our daily lives. Am not leaving alone their spouses too who could play a significant role in their decisions.

All the chapters are independent of itself. They are not very much interconnected. I have made a conscious effort to ensure that you do not feel overwhelmed on the topics. I have started off with a brief history of the data in the first chapter and how the data explosion has happened over the past few decades. In the second chapter, I have discussed on the future of food. What could be the options for food for the future? Later in the third and fourth chapters, the discussions have been centered on the new technologies that would change the way we see our financial world - the bit coin and the ethereum platforms. Following that, I have shared the prospects of the emerging technology Goliaths and how these technology companies will change our future lifestyle. The sixth chapter is more on my thoughts on how human race shaped the world and how is it shaping the new world. Going forward in the seventh chapter, there is a discussion on how the medical field could emerge with the new breakthroughs in biotechnology. In the eighth chapter, I have discussed one of the hot topics of the century - how automation is changing the world economy? The chapter also discusses multiple phases of technology transformation. The final chapter discusses on how the Maslow's hierarchy of earth is changing according to the priorities of the dominant race.

Finally, I have addressed a few areas of technology in which a potential investor or entrepreneur could focus. Although this is not a comprehensive analysis or dissertation on everything an investor or entrepreneur needs to know about the future of opportunities, I've tried to include a few important perspectives that I think they must pay attention to. The humble efforts to consolidate my thoughts could not have been possible without the help of my parents, friends, colleagues, professors, and family (my wife Mary, and my three daughters Sneha, Shreya and Sera). The credit for the photos and illustrations goes to Isha Lakhani. I do owe my credit to Pohar from Partridge Publishing and to my friend Arun James Sebastian who has helped me in reviewing my writings.

THE DATA THEORY
OF CHATQUAKE

S ome silly things do happen in life. I was desperately looking for my wedding photographs to prepare a romantic album for my wife over the last weekend, considering my impending wedding anniversary. I initially thought of digging out old photographs and making a collage and gifting it to her. Since I am a decently disorganised person, I had to hunt for the album overnight. I was dumbstruck to see that the thin films of the transparent separators in the album had already made a natural collage of the photographs. I could realise the convenience the bankruptcy of Kodak had brought into our lives. The lack of exaptation by Kodak has resulted in New Age cameras that I still love to use anytime, and those come with the luxury of clicking photographs with ease and obviously at zero cost.

From the time when George Eastman put the first simple camera into the hands of consumers in 1888, with the slogan 'you press the button, we do the rest', to the technology of LinX Imaging that is used in Apple for multiple aperture photography, the world has transformed into data than a simple photograph. Not only these have technologies changed the way of Kodak moment (a moment worthy of capturing with a photograph, especially an adorable moment, which was a marketing tactic of the Kodak), they also have knocked down the exclusive privilege of a photographer. The accuracy of capturing such moments using the camera transformed more into the capability of the hardware and the software used in the camera than the individual skill. So, what did we lose in this transition? Is it the ethos of the photography, or is it the skill that had been preserved for generations?

In those thoughts, I cautiously removed the photographs that were stuck to each other. The silver iodide on the photos has given those photos a halo feel. But over the next few generations, do we see such a halo feel on the old photographs? Yes, we would find such exquisite art pieces mostly in Smithsonian Institute and possibly in some private collections of millionaires. In the camera expo conducted by Canon where the focus is to give a glimpse of the future of camera technology, the company had showcased a camera that obviously cannot be used for taking selfie—a whole nicer mammoth of 250 megapixel and a perfect night vision camera that would work on 4,000,000 ISO (International Standards Organization: the lower the ISO number, the less sensitive the instrument is to the light, while a higher ISO number increases the sensitivity). These would again explode the visual data on the net.

Just to quote, KPCB analyst, Mary Meeker's, annual Internet trends report states that all Internet-connected citizens share over 1.8 billion photos each day. With the massive number of images that are being generated through Facebook, Snapchat, WhatsApp, Instagram, and other similar apps, the quantum of image data is unimaginable. I recently read in the IDC reports that by 2020, we would be having 44 zettabytes (trillion gigabytes) of data in the public Internet domain. If we stack iPads around the earth for so much content, which is enough data to fill 30 billion 64GB Apple iPads if stacked well, it would be over sixty stacks around the earth. To give a growth perspective, in 2011, we created around 1.8 zettabytes (or 1.8 trillion GB) of information. That, itself, is enough to build a Great iPad Wall of China. In 2012, it reached 2.8 zettabytes, and now we are aimed to generate 44 zettabytes (ZB) by 2020. But anyway, I had limited time for these thoughts to process in my mind because it was my anniversary, and the amount of data that our world would be having in 2020 would be the last thing my wife would need to hear from me.

OMG! I had to find an alternative way to get something of sentimental value to her. I decided to hunt for my hard disk to get some pictures of our 'good old days'. I was blessed with the soft copies that I found on the hard disk. I was so thankful to IBM for introducing this secondary storage device. Though I haven't seen a hard disk from IBM, I had seen them in exhibitions. These original drives from IBM came in a size of approximately the size of two refrigerators and stored around 3.75 MB. Just imagine if we were using such hard disks for our personal use in our computers. To give a perspective, any hi-tech household would have a 1TB hard disk, which would need a room that would accommodate 54,000 refrigerators to store such amount of data. In the modern world, that would count to a 100-storey building to store the data of a single household. I pay my complete respect to the people who worked day in, day out to compress such refrigerators and gave me a cute little hard disk.

Coming back to my household, the happiness of finding my hard disk didn't last long. My little daughter grabbed the disk from my hand to get hold of the *Tom and Jerry* collection, and there it goes to the ground. I didn't know what to say! There lie my whole collection of songs, photographs, videos, and movies I had collected over past few years. I had some hope to connect and check the data. I could just hear a ticking sound from the hard disk. It was all over. More than my loss, my daughter was disappointed to see her *Tom and Jerry* collection go down the drain.

To my curiosity, she asked me whether she could make the series of such collection so that if someone lost such videos, she could provide those videos. I had to explain to her how the entertainment through the cartoons evolved. It took me a long time to make her understand the mechanics of such an evolved entertainment tool, and how the future of this industry would look in next decade.

Actually, what is a cartoon? Is it just a visual art that just a combination of few lines, or it is the expression of humanity for whom it is being designed for? Even though the entertainment through drawings were done through Bayeux Tapestry, a 70-metre embroidered cloth that depicts the events in the English country, the origin of this as an industry saw its rising in the nineteenth century. The word evolved from the word

'Karton', describing a heavy paperboard, found its use in the production of frescoes in the early nineteenth century. In the later part of the century, satirical humour occupied the newspapers and the magazines of England. The favourite topics for these cartoons were mostly political. It was a shy, self-deprecating, and insecure man, Walt Disney, who changed the perspective of children's entertainment through cartoons. From Mickey Mouse to the latest avatars of Captain America, the cartoon characters not only depicted the identity of America but also introduced an American dream to the little minds of the third world. With the power of YouTube, the freedom to express has driven this industry to a digital world with digital characters. It may be beautifully weird as *Ben10* and entirely digital like *Dick Figures* or *Simon's Cat*.

Our children have to start appreciating such New Age cartoons than the ones those had the touch of living creatures. But I have noticed that the children also appreciate those changes. They have started appreciating short YouTube shows than the older Mickeys, the Toms, and the Jerrys.

This trend is not just with the kids. Even with the adults, people have started appreciating videos more than the written and pictographic content. This gives a huge impetus for the digital video content in the years to come. With the augmented and virtual reality, this space would see an unimaginable twist. According to

Cisco, by 2019, around 80 per cent of the global Internet traffic would be video content, and that too on edutainment segment. The content that would be generated in a month, according to this statistic, would take an average person around five million years to watch. There would be intelligent applications that would recommend videos based on demographic analytics.

In the next five years, half of the world population will be having access to the Internet through handheld devices. According to Pyramid Research, this increase alone will soar mobile video usage at a compound annual growth rate of 28 per cent over the next five years. This would again transform the way in which we appreciate the content too; the current television content would migrate to a video-streaming-based viewership.

Whatever said and done to address my problem at hand, I started to search for an online secondary data storage. As our data transfer speeds increase, to the current record of 1.125 TB per second by the optical communication developed by University College London, my entire hard disk could be downloaded in less than a second. If I have an online cloud storage, then my data is perpetual. I was happy!

Even though this technology may take a few years to commercialise, considering the explosion of the storage economics that would thrash the Moore's law (the number of transistors in a dense integrated circuit doubles approximately every two years), I believe the dialogue on DNA storage was much more impressive for a common man like me. The kind of progress that humanity had from our era of floppies to the latest DNA storages devices, which may be our own bodies, no sooner than later, blew my mind off. I had to pinch myself when I came across the work in which DNA suspended in water is used for data storage.

To give a perspective of DNA, around one-tenth of a million molecules of DNA can be fit into the width of a hair. Literally, the library of congress can be fit into a few strands of hair. I remember around four years back; I had read a news that scientists successfully stored 5.5 petabytes of data in a gram of DNA. That's equivalent to 700 1TB hard disks. The research over the past few years must have taken this number that would need a few minutes to count the zeros at the end. With a new technique developed by University of Washington and Microsoft, the space needed to store digital data that today would fill a Walmart supercentre could be stored in a space of a sugar cube through the DNA storage technology. Some interesting information could follow based on the calculations provided by Bitesize Bio, a bioscientist's blog. If we ignore all non-human cells that live in our body and focus only on the cells that make up our body, it would range anywhere between 10 trillion and 100 trillion. If we take 100 trillion cells as the generally accepted estimate, and each cell contains 1.5 GB of data, the approximate amount of data that can be stored in the human body is 150 zettabytes (10^{21}). (Assuming a single DNA has two strands with three billion base pairs grouped into twenty-three chromosomes represents a single genome contains about 6×10^9 base pairs.)

Moreover, with such simple mechanics, I was quite sure that I need not fear the loss of data. I am glad that my wedding photos can be stored for more than 1,000 years. But can we transform the data storage to a service that can be seamlessly accessible? I think we can. Even if we do it, what would we do with such a large quantum of information? It would be a daunting question for a technology leader who is planning to use such data for enhanced client experiences. As a way, there are consulting services that would recommend the firms how it should run the business. Considering the amount of data getting generated in the world, soon there would be recommender apps and content that would guide the common man on what to read, listen, and write. Let's see what is happening to our services industry.

As we see, the industry is getting transformed or, rather, I would put that the burgeoning clusters of startups are transforming such client experience. Since I had been a career banker and technology enthusiast, I always get excited about money and technology. Let's take a simple example of banking. Why are (or were, possibly it has come down drastically) we going to banks? Is it just the matter of money? I think people never banked with an institution just for money. They banked to have a trusted companion and a feeling of support (from the perspective of money). With the emergence of the modern technology, we lost a little bit of personal touch on such relationships. I don't think you would have met your chic relationship manager at the bank personally (I haven't). There are banks that charge if you try to do that.

Anyway, how would we be able to bring back that personal touch for the banking or, for that matter, any other services with the New Age technologies? But can we convey the personal touch by any other means and method? I would say that to recreate any experience, modern technology has to do a simple activity. It just needs to stimulate all five senses and give us an illusion that we are in a real world. Isn't that the real world or a real virtual reality? With the arrival of Oculus Rift by the end of 2016, the concept conceptualised by Ivan Sutherland will emerge into a new dimension. It could be the next wonderland into which Alice would walk into—it would be the possibility of walking into the constructs of the imagination. This transforms the boundaries of the Internet from two-dimensional to three-dimensional that would change the perception of human mind.

There are some industries that are relatively untouched by the evolution of the Internet, such as real estate, healthcare, school education, travel and tourism, apparels, etc. The VR is expected to transform every segment of such industries and make such things virtually accessible. I presume everyone remembers the launch of hit mobile game Pokemon Go made by Niantic, a gaming portal based out of San Francisco. This game is an example of how VR can be seamlessly integrated into our environment to give such a realistic picture of our surroundings that our senses believe the experiences to be true. This is termed as the augmented reality specifically designed to add and enhance the things you do as a human being: Being outside, socializing with other people, shopping, playing, having fun. Augmented reality can make all those experiences better. Imagine you try out your home with the virtual replicas of your belongings, and customise the home accordingly. With innovations such as the Facebook's Oculus, Microsoft's HoloLens, Google's Magic Leap and Glass, the market looks like it lacks a disruptive leader. Once a company like Apple launches a cost-effective experience in the virtual reality world, as projected by Digi-Capital, the market would reach 150 billion dollars by 2020.

Again, from the perspective of data, virtual reality would be the right tool to analyse the quantum of data that is being produced, as discussed earlier. As his personal assistant, Jarvis responds to Tony Stark to make the rational decisions through highly effective artificial intelligence in the movie *Ironman*. One day, we can imagine a personal virtual assistant who could help us more effectively in decision-making. I believe that it would be a blessing for me, at this point in time, for such an adviser to recommend the ideal solution to solve my current problem at hand—to give an anniversary gift to my wife.

From the time when Pamela McCordick quoted the wish of humanity to forge the gods to the time now when David Levy has envisioned in his book, *Love and Sex with Robots*, that marrying robots will be normal by 2050, artificial intelligence has evolved beyond imagination. This would result in a similar debate that was all set in the twenty-first century in the name of cloning. Whatever is said and done, the emotional experience of such a robot when he or she discovers that it is just a merchandise and has no right to live may bring in tears for at least a few.

So coming back to the question of how the service industry is going to evolve would be a question that would haunt any firm aspiring to design the consumer-centric front end for their product. Let's analyse various mediums of service deliveries that used to serve men and women. As the modern economy developed, humans moved away from manufacturing of goods industry that included agriculture, mining, manufacturing, and construction. These activities created some kind of tangible objects. But when the civilisation evolved, humanity transformed itself into a service society.

Though the early service that was adopted by mankind was prostitution, later, all sorts of services were initiated with the start of trade. In the modern economy, we come across banking, telecommunications, engineering services, computer services, medicine, and consumer and government services such as defence and administration of justice. In the early part of twentieth century, only 30 per cent of the workforce was in service, and the rest were in agriculture and manufacturing; but by the beginning of the twenty-first century, 80 per cent of the jobs were in the service industry. The key industries that have shown the most progress are business services, social services, and healthcare services. The way in which the wave of automation washed away the manufacturing sector, it is possible that the new communication platforms based on mobile devices would make disruptive changes to the existing service channels.

The first description of the social interactions that could be enabled through networking was by Licklider of MIT in 1962, discussing his 'Galactic Network' concept. The Internet was based on this idea proposed by him and his peers at DARPA that there would be multiple independent networks of rather arbitrary design, conceptualising the mother of the current Internet as we see it named as the ARPANET. Algorithms that enabled smooth communications through packet switching and efficient networking were the fundamentals of Internet. The contract given to Stanford, BBN, and UCLA by DARPA to implement the TCP/IP protocol was the beginning of long-term experimentation and development of Internet concepts.

Right from the first generation industrial revolution by steam engine, second generation by electricity, third by the development of Internet, we are entering the fourth generation of industrial revolution through digital, physical, and biological interfaces. In the coming era, it would be difficult to identify what is natural and what is artificial. One of the key drivers would be the transformation of the communication platforms as we see them. 'With the emergence of Internet marketing' was the buzzword for the previous decade.

It all started with the email in 1983 when CompuServe launched the first Internet touchpoint as a product for the users of a specific service. A decade later, in 1993, Tim Berners Lee's hypertext protocol was available as a browser by the name Mosaic, which became Netscape Navigator. This was the birth of the digital interactive marketing and advertising as we've come to know it.

The advent of Amazon by Jeff Bezos in 1995 marked the launch of e-commerce. The rules of the market started changing with the emergence of handheld devices' advertising platforms by Apple in 2007 with the launch of iPhone. The emergence of social media platforms with LinkedIn in 2002, Yelp in 2004, and Facebook in 2004 took off the social media side of the Internet. As of now, an American spends around eleven hours online, and two-thirds of the population check their mobile devices for Internet.

Going forward, Vint Cerf, one of the founding fathers of the Internet, envisions having interplanetary Internet too. Before we get there, let's see why it is wise for service sector companies to consider the new emerging bot platforms as the game changers. In the supersaturated digital economy where the website and mobile app are taken for granted for any business, the emergence of the bot economy would be a silver lining. Humans, being social and connected, have time to spend over 300 minutes in a week in connecting and chatting with those connections through the popular chat applications, such as Facebook Messenger and WhatsApp. For Facebook, this opportunity will open up a new way of business to reach users via a chat interface. But is this going to be scalable? Is it going to be the next big market, or is it just a hype?

I desperately need someone to talk to check what women want. Should I do a Google, or should I chat with a friend? I would take the latter option now, since it gives me the comfort that I am taking a decision based on human reasoning rather than just the data available on a search engine. So is it a bot I'm looking for? And how much better can I use it? They are apps that would enable the users to interact through textual or conversational interfaces rather than the traditional click to action kind of interfaces. It would take us one step towards the machine intelligence that would understand what you would say, and then respond (which has been the idea behind developing the computer program by Alan Turing).

The bot may not be a completely new concept. It is the New Age version of billboards or chat rooms from the times of ActiveBuddy's Smarterchild (later taken over by AOL). The way Smarterchild developed intimate friendships with over thirty million instant messenger users and over a billion messages a day, these New Age bots would change the way of human interaction with the computer. But what could change or has changed from now and then?

Smarterchild was an intelligent bot developed by ActiveBuddy, and it was widely distributed across instant messaging platforms after it was founded in 2000. This chatterbot acted as a showcase for fun-based personalised conversations. This was a flourishing business model, but when it got acquired by Microsoft, they decided to kill this product. In many ways, Smarterchild was the pre-curser to our current Siri and Cortana. Considering the evolution of the new platform, two factors, as I see, would aid the revival of such chatterbox platforms—the growth of measurable data and the growth of the Internet and mobile technologies. To put the data explosion/generation in context, every minute of every day we create more than 204 million email messages, over two million Google search queries, forty-eight hours of new YouTube videos, 684,000 bits of content is shared on Facebook.

When we know the user muscle of these messaging apps is headed to two billion users globally, which are around 30 per cent of the global population in 2016, what would happen if we are able to chat to a bot without even knowing that the discussion is done with a machine? The beauty of the opportunity lies in refining the Natural Language Processing or NLP capability. Instead of a monotonous IVR, we hear the pleasant voice of a Siri/Cortana and get into a discussion on a topic of our interest. So what is Natural Language Processing? It dates back even to the times of

Leibniz and Descartes of the seventeenth century when they put across proposals to convert words between languages. The turning point of this technology came when Alan Turing published the article on *Computing Machinery and Intelligence* that proposed the Turing test, which evaluated the ability of a computer program to impersonate a human in a real-time written conversation.

Later, with the syntactic structures devised by Noam Chomsky, the universal grammar evolved leading to the foundation of statistical machine translation algorithms. IBM has been one of the forerunners in this field of language processing. The latest avatar of the language processing is the question answering machine, Watson by IBM, built with machine retrieval of knowledge and machine learning and reasoning. Even though the research on NLP was focused on English (Watson was specifically developed to answer questions on the quiz show, Jeopardy), it will soon expand to other languages too to address the local crowd.

We are talking about a 'chatquake' in countries, especially in India where we already have an average millennial (aged 16–30 years) spending about 2.2 hours a day (or about thirty-four days in a year) on their mobile devices. This technology would transform the world of healthcare by developing global evidence-based learning capabilities, allowing it to function as a clinical diagnostics and decision system. It will also find refined applications in the education sector by creating virtual assistants for students in the emerging economies where there is a dearth of quality teachers.

Once we build the expertise to integrate these technologies, it will catalyse the click market transformation to a chat market. You could be conversing with an app rather than swiping over the phone. This would increase the local marketing and user engagement, and reduce customer support and interaction costs. On the flip side, this transition may not come cheap. The firms planning to enter transformation would need support from platforms such as IBM, Facebook, and Google that would charge for the privilege of talking to their customers and using their algorithms. This may open up a bot economy parallel to the app economy and, in turn, open up another channel for client services. This space has been revolutionised by the launch of a bot platform by Facebook. With the big data analytics, the quantum of data that's being generated exponentially, and with the intelligence that we would be able to program into the bots through analytics on human thoughts, the bots will be as much part of our conversation as real people are.

Who knows for my next anniversary, a bot would recommend me another bot that I could gift to my wife on my behalf. Need to wait and see.

IS THE FUTURE OF THE FOOD WE EAT STILL A MYSTERY?

I was looking forward to spending the Easter weekend with my family. After three months of working without a vacation, the thought of doing absolutely nothing for six days was really exciting for me. 'Wow!' The aroma of the Robusta coffee that I had bought from the so-called sustainable coffee orchards of Wayanad had filled my room early in the morning on Easter Sunday. I just woke up, and scanned through the newspapers and saw my wife busy in preparing our family breakfast for the Easter Sunday. Since the whole family was around, she wanted to have the breakfast made with the traditional puttu and kadala (Bengal gram) curry, along with the traditional appam and beef curry (as the end of lent) of Kerala, one of the top breakfast dishes in the world.

Pleased with the gastronomical delight she had offered for the breakfast, I decided to give her a break by taking the family for a family dinner that night. In the voting for the venue, she and our elder daughter voted in favour of the traditional Japanese restaurant—one of her favourite restaurants. We went to the beach in the evening, and got primed up for the grand dinner. While at the beach, my younger daughter started getting cranky about the venue of the dinner. She wanted a fast food joint that would give her some freebies as toys and some sheets to paint rather than a fine dining restaurant. But I wanted my wife to have a pleasant environment so that she could unwind from the

15

hectic preparations for the holy week. Half an hour of debate, the 'chauvinist' wins.

I made up my mind to take the side of my wife and the elder daughter, as usual, and the decision was final—the same Japanese restaurant. I pre-booked the table on the way and opted for a river-facing one. We reached the restaurant, and our regular waiter came to us with a warm smile. He presented the menu and mentioned that the restaurant has started the Yakiniku, one of the full-fledged Japanese steaks. We were curious to see how it tasted and decided to order one. Since the order was freshly made, according to the waiter, we had to wait for twenty minutes before the dish came. Instead of breaking the ice with chit-chat, I didn't know why my elder daughter asked me a question that made me think a little bit about the food that we were going to eat. The question was really simple, 'Daddy, why do we eat cooked food rather than uncooked or pounded meat?' My immediate answer was that it helps with a better digestion, kills bacteria, and adds flavour, but it directed me to a different thought on how humans started to differentiate between the food and the dishes. In order to learn about the origins of cooking, I delved into the origins of human settlement, and the motivation of mankind to develop the economics and chemistry of food.

Spending a few weeks on this topic, whenever I got time from my schedule, I could understand that there were several episodes in the gastronomical evolution of the mankind. From the times we understood what to eat and how to eat, we had always been 'in pursuit of happiness' that we always got through gluttony (can be a lighter word too). To understand the uniqueness of the evolution of food, and how the food that we eat today evolved, I had to scan through various topics on hunting, agriculture, and war. When I delved into the history of food, four key inventions came out as important milestones in its history. 'The evolution of spear', 'use of fire', 'development of agriculture', 'invention of plough and agricultural chemicals and, hence, the industrialisation' were the four milestones that changed the way in which we eat food. As Voltaire once said about the consumption of food, 'Nothing would be more tiresome than eating and drinking if God had not made them a pleasure as well as a necessity.' So how and when did we make the activity of food consumption a pleasurable activity?

Throughout the vast majority of human history, we acquired our food either by hunting wild animals like mammoths, rhinos, and elks or by gathering food from wild plants. Though not by choice, our ancestors ate wild fruits, vegetables, protein, and fat. The 'evolution of the spear' into a tensioned bow and an arrow was a very critical invention for the existence of mankind at that time, and thus collection of food. The realisation that a pointed object could kill a fast approaching animal, way back at least 500,000 years ago, paved the way for a new era for mankind. The invention of stone-tipped spears-hafting in the following years was a significant point in human evolution that allowed our forefathers to kill animals more efficiently and have more regular access to meat, which they would have needed to feed ever-growing brains. This technique not only helped them to think and plan ahead; it helped them to develop skills to haft the stone tools to the wooden shaft as a composite technology.

Possibly without the invention of spears, we could be yet another species of mammals that may be always on a hunt for food. With the help of these tools, the volume of the food gathered increased exponentially that forced us to think, and thus made us explore the ways and means to preserve food such as drying and smoking. The process of food production in Paleolithic times was simple—consisting of gathering, hunting, and fishing. This composite technology not only gave our ancestors an easier way to kill the prey but also helped them to make the kill from a distance of around 10 to 30 metres.

With the onset of the Neolithic Revolution, new food-producing skills were devised with new set of tools—such as crude ploughs, stone sickles, and stone querns that ground the grains—were devised to serve the needs of agriculture and animal husbandry. Conscious effort of efficiency, precision, and accuracy started a little late when man started in the Bronze Age (3350–3100 BC) with the advent of agriculture.

The use of composite materials not only changed the way of hunting but also changed the way of eating too. Even though there is no definite timeline for the use of knife and cutlery, knife-like tools had been used at least two and a half million years ago, and evidences for its use have been found at the site of Olduvai Gorge in Tanzania. From the times the food was the need for humans, the spoons had been there with them. Something to scoop it up had always been a requirement. Even though the natural spoons could have been made with humble beginnings with the seashells and naturally curved stones, the evidence of the usage of spoons with handles was found among the Egyptians around 1000 BC—made with slate, wood, flint, and ivory.

In the New Age, the Romans and the Greeks used the metal cutlery made of bronze and silver. The modern business of cutlery can be divided between the premium and the disposable segments. To compare the business from an ecological perspective, it would be interesting to look at the business of modern spears from the damages it made on earth through the waste they generated. The premium segment of cutlery made of metals does not generate the garbage to the size of garbage produced by plastic cutlery, since such cutlery can be recycled. Every year, just the numbers from US estimate that 40 billion pieces of plastic cutlery end up in the garbage. In emerging markets, like India, it is much more than the estimates of US. It is over 120 billion pieces annually. The thought of reducing this plastic dump has motivated a few individuals in the emerging market to transform the cutlery to be edible. The companies such as Bakey's have made a breakthrough by making edible spoons with sorghum, rice, and wheat flour—the new-generation consumable spears. It is completely vegan, has no preservatives, and is both trans-fat and dairy-free. As we move to the future, with the focus of such startups, it may so happen that the result of an era-long evolution of cutlery may transform into something that we can 'just eat'.

Coming back to the core thoughts that I gave to my kid on the evolution of the food, I believe the second milestone will be the use of fire. Although we all have heard about the sufferings of Prometheus from the Hellenic mythology for providing human race the gift of fire from Mt. Olympus, the first evidence of early humans using fire dates back to more than a million years. The practice did not become routine until about 650,000 years later. Man must have gone through a number of accidents before he realised that even if the fire is a devastating force, it can be tamed and be used for getting heat and light, and, above all, can be used for cooking.

By the mid-Pleistocene era (2,588,000 to 11,700 years ago), he began to preserve the power of fire from wherever he could encounter—from the bush fires or from the acts of God. The ability to control and manipulate fire has contributed to the development of the human brain. With the advent of the controlled fire, human activity was no longer restricted to the times of sunlight. This increased the time for human to think and become confident against the predators he had been facing since the time of evolution. A lot of inventions started happening in parallel with the idea to tame fire—the modern man was getting moulded. He started to build houses (around 10,000 BC in Jericho) to stay at, and staying indoors directed him to develop calendars based on moon. He started carving the phases of the moon with bones and pointed spears. The development of housing indirectly made the nomadic man to settle and organise to form a society. The settlement, thus, started as a result of the social network that was getting formed and gave way to agriculture around 8000 BC, resulting in the development of great civilisations as we know today.

So how did fire help us in developing intelligence? The key advantage of fire was that when food got cooked, the complex carbohydrates in foods became more digestible and allowed humans to absorb more food energy per unit of food consumed. This could possibly be the reason that we evolved into a specie that have brains averaging a bit larger than 1,000 ml, twice the size of chimpanzee skulls, which have 400 ml, and gorillas, which have 600 ml.

At this stage of evolution, our cultural and linguistic complexity and technological prowess took a significant leap forward. The better nutrient absorbent capabilities developed by human body—resulting from better-cooked food—catalysed our brains to grow to accommodate such changes. If this transformation has not happened, we would have been a refined dinosaur with a large volume of the brain, but less evolved.

So what changed in our body as a result of the fire? The human digestive system evolved to deal with cooked foods and, hence, developed a refined body. Cooking would also explain the increase in hominid brain sizes, shorter digestive tracts, smaller teeth and jaws. The refinement of cooking increased the variety of food that could be prepared by a human, and thus develop the modern sense of taste.

Previously, indigestible components of plants, such as raw plant cellulose and starch from stems, mature leaves, enlarged roots, and tubers, became part of a staple diet for the human civilisation. The key impact was on meat. Cooking the meat acted as a form of 'predigestion', allowing less energy to be spent on digesting the tougher proteins such as collagen. As a result, the digestive tract shrank, allowing more energy to be given to the growing brain. To give a perspective, if humans ate only raw and unprocessed food, humans would need to eat for 9.3 hours per day in order to fuel their brains. Our brains use about twice as much resting energy (energy used the by brain when it is resting) by percentage as other primates, an advantage that gave a huge edge for humans to develop the brains over the rest of the primates.

Let's see how cooking has given advantage to our digestive system. It was the work of Rachel Carmody that threw light on the digestion process of the uncooked food. According to her, there is growing evidence that we overstate the energy extracted by the body from whole raw foods. She explains that only a fraction of calories in raw starch and protein are absorbed by the body directly through the small intestine. The balance of the food passes through a large bowel where it is broken down by microbes into smaller molecules that can be absorbed. The cost these microbes take is that they consume the lion's share of such cracked-down molecules, which leaves a small fraction of the raw food to be absorbed by the human body. Cooked food, by contrast, is mostly digested by the time it enters the colon. To give a perspective of the nutrient absorption, the body gets roughly 30 per cent more energy from cooked oat, wheat, or potato starch as compared to raw, and as much as 78 per cent from the protein in an egg. This should be enough for us to understand the power of fire and how it changed the physical and intellectual capabilities of the human.

Today, when I reach to a light switch in the middle the of the night, I do not realise that until the invention of electric light, humans had to work with the fire and oil to lighten the darkness—a discovery that enabled the human beings to lengthen the day and helped them to become much smarter. We finished the dinner by the time I explained these topics to my daughter. Then she was curious to know why we started to settle, domesticate animals, and start agriculture. Being not an easy question, I decided to do more research before I could give her a convincing answer. On the way back, I asked my wife to take the car for me so that I could read about the importance of agriculture in our lives.

From as early as 11,000 BC, humans began a gradual transition from a hunter-gatherer towards cultivating crops and rearing animals for food. 'The shift to agriculture', the third milestone, happened in both the Fertile Crescent, a region in the Middle East, and at Chogha Golan in modern-day Iran. Independent development of agriculture happened in China, Africa, New Guinea, India, and Americas too. By 6,000 BC, the Fertile Crescent, the land running from Syria and Palestine towards the delta of Euphrates, Tigris, and the Nile, started to emerge; this emergence is considered as the cradle of modern civilisation—the Garden of Eden. In the country between the rivers, Mesopotamia, the human settlements started to emerge, and man started to use plants that are suitable for soil and climate. Fields were set up in the fertile deltas of the rivers, and the regulated supply of water emerged. The development of early civilisation, thus, is closely connected with the invention of irrigation. This has not changed even in the modern era. Even today, most of the developed settlements still thrive in the sides of fresh water bodies. Around 5,000 BC, cultivation of rice flourished in the Indian subcontinent with the usage of plough. In the similar lines, the Mesopotamian civilisation also gained ground in the development of agriculture as we see in the modern times.

So what motivated human for this transition to organised living compared to that of nomads? It could be related to changes in climate that caused the shortage of food or baby boom, or could be the surge in weather resulting in denser populations that demanded more food, or maybe the domestication of animals and plants seemed to be more reliable source of supply of food than they could get from the wild, and thus changing lifestyle. No matter what motivated this change in lifestyle, it created the oldest industry in the world—the agriculture that has a current output of over seven trillion dollars annually that feeds over 70 per cent of the people worldwide and employs over 75 per cent of the world population. This was quite a large number for my kid to understand. Still, she could appreciate how agriculture transformed our society as we see today.

Even though agricultural techniques such as irrigation, crop rotation, etc. evolved, the major breakthrough happened with the 'industrialisation of agriculture', which was the fourth milestone. The invention of tools, such as plough, helped to make the land more fertile. The earliest farm improvement technique was the use of plough, a crude pointed bent stick or tree branch, which was used to stir the soil surface. It soon became apparent that more the soil was stirred or tilled, the better the germination and crop quality. Man continually strived to become more efficient. With this drive, he developed handheld hoes, and thus developed simple ploughs to till his land.

The early Egyptians did the evolutionary discovery over 4,000 years ago. Later, oxen, camels, elephants, and in some cases, even humans were used to pull these primitive ploughs. Animals enabled the land to be tilled more easily and faster, thus, producing more food. This was not enough to bring a better yield. In the process to boost the output and protect the produce from pests, we tried various chemicals that were available handy for us. That varied from the use of salt to even the dung to improve the crop productivity, and to keep away the pests. This need was satiated by the use of elemental sulphur—first known pesticide used for dusting in Mesopotamia (the Sumerians) about 4,500 years ago. Later, mercury and arsenical compounds were used in Asia to control pests.

Gradually, the chemical combinations such as Bordeaux mixture, a combination of copper sulphate and lime, emerged. The true change happened with the invention of ammonium nitrate synthesis through Haber-Bosch method, and the DDT by Dr Paul Muller in the first half of twentieth century. These inventions helped mankind to revolutionise the agricultural production (cereals alone) and reach the output of over 2,500 million tonnes in 2015.

Let's explore how the progress of human race, by mastering the techniques of production and consumption of food, impacted our earth. If we take the case of arable land, the land that can be ploughed and used for crops, one-third of such land is used for agriculture. Out of such land, over 70 per cent of the land is used for grazing and growing only meat. Is this an efficient way to harness the productivity of nature?

On the consumption side, we have a few concerns that need immediate attention. By 2050, the world's population is predicted to hit 9.7 billion people from 7.3 billion today—an addition of 2.7 billion people to feed. To give a perspective, 200,000 people are added to the demand every day, particularly in Asia, China, India, and Southeast Asia. The food demand is expected to increase at least by 60 per cent for cereals and 85 per cent for meat (according to World Bank). To add to this trend, there is a clear shift in the pattern of food consumption. The per capita meat and milk consumption is also growing—especially in China and India—and is projected to remain high in the European Union, North America, Brazil, and Russia. These foods are much more resource-intensive to produce than plant-based diets. So can we blame the efficiency of existing agricultural distribution network? If yes, we just need to evenly distribute the world production of food.

According to World Resource Institute, even if we took all the food produced in 2009, and distributed it evenly among the global population, the world will still need to produce 974 more calories per person per day by 2050. Taking into account the current production rates, our current agricultural output will not meet the projected demand of the world.

By the time I explained these thoughts to my kids, we had reached home after having the Yakiniku. I had taken the delivery menu of the restaurant to get a sense of the dishes they had. I was surprised to see their claim on the menu that the restaurant used meat only from sustainable sources. I wondered what would define the sustainability of food consumption, especially meat. I was curious to understand how the food menu will look twenty years from now. In the modern era of culinary laboratories, such as El Buli and fine dining chefs from Michelin's, how will we refine the science of gastronomy? Should we be a little more sensitive about the methods of sustainable agriculture?

The post–world war food demand, agricultural progress in developed countries, and green revolution (not so sure whether we should call it a red revolution or green revolution) encouraged the insensitive use of fertilisers and pesticides in agriculture. These contributed one-third of freshwater pollution with elements such as phosphorus and nitrogen. Agriculture contributes nearly one-quarter of global greenhouse gas emissions, uses one-third of landmass (excluding Antarctica), and accounts for three-fourth of all freshwater withdrawn from rivers, lakes, and aquifers—one hundred times more than we use for personal needs. This would accelerate the water stress and desertification resulting in global warming, and thus reducing the acreage of arable land available for agriculture every year.

The insensitive usage of hybrid and GM crops and look out for efficient farming resulted in the several native varieties of fruits and vegetables disappearing, and giving way to a few varieties that made better economic sense for large-scale cultivation. For instance, four out of five North American apple varieties are on the brink of vanishing. Red Delicious, one of the most common varieties seen in our supermarkets, accounts for more than 40 per cent of the apples grown in the United States, leaving traditional varieties less and less likely to be crunched by future generations. The highly acclaimed 'positive effects' of the green revolution are levelling-off, considering the shrinkage of gene pool and pests getting increasingly resistant to disease. The benefit of this transition is mainly harvested by the Monsantos and the Potashcorps of the world.

How can we change this trend? As per the projections of Food and Agriculture Organisation, the global demand for food would be spread over five types of specific food. Over 50 per cent of our consumption would be cereals, oils would account for 10 per cent, meat and sugar would be another 7– 8 per cent individually, and the tubers would account for another 5 per cent. The major impact of the cost of production will be with the slightest increase in the demand for meat.

To give an idea of the cost it takes to produce meat: on an average, it takes roughly seven kilograms of grain to be consumed to produce a one kilogram gain in live weight. For pork, the figure is close to four kilograms of grain per kilogram of weight gain; for poultry, it is just over two; and for herbivorous species of farmed fish (such as carp, tilapia, and catfish), it is less than two. It is projected that meat consumption will increase from 37.4 kg/person/year in 2000 to 52 kg/person/year translating to 455 million metric tonnes of meat in 2050. This explosive growth will take a toll on the production of cereal production, since more than 50 per cent of the cereal production is routed to increase the meat production. Dramatic changes in the consumption patterns of protein-rich food in emerging economies, such as China and India, are going to catalyse the slaughter of livestock day by day.

Do we have an alternate to meat? In 1931, Winston Churchill said a possibility of growing meat in an industrial setting, 'We shall escape the absurdity of growing a whole chicken in order to eat the breast or wing by growing these parts separately under a suitable medium.' It took another eighty-one years to make this a reality when a Dutchman team from Maastricht University gave a demonstration of in vitro beef burger in London. They developed it by taking muscle cells and applying a protein that promotes tissues' growth. They claim that under ideal conditions, in two months, in vitro meat could deliver up to 50,000 tonnes of meat from ten pork muscle cells. Wow! Quite an achievement. If we are unable to cope with the growing demand for the meat, we may need to completely rely on in vitro meat.

Even though creative ideas like lab-grown meat, 3D-printed food on request, and the meal in a pill are still in the labs with exorbitantly expensive bills—such technologies will be the way forward for coming generations. The concoction of algae and living tissue from a livestock currently brews in a sugar scaffolding at a cost of US$32500 to make a piece of burger-sized meat. Can the brew be a little cheaper with a larger scale? Something yet to be seen. Backed by Google Ventures and Bill Gates, startups such as Impossible Foods and Beyond Meat are betting on burgers and chicken strips made from plant-based substitutes like soybeans and grains.

But are we utilising the food that's being produced to the optimum? Another interesting anomaly to note is that 20 per cent of food produced or harvested is lost, owing to insufficient processing, storage, and transport. To give a perspective, every day, around 4.4 million apples, 5.1 million potatoes, 2.8 million tomatoes, and 1.6 million bananas are thrown away as waste. This is not just a waste of produce but also is a loss of the factors of production. The wastage happens at all steps of production, handling, storage, processing, distribution, and consumption. This wastage has huge impact. Without accounting for greenhouse gas emissions, the carbon footprint of the food produced and not eaten is estimated at 3.3 gigatons of carbon dioxide equivalent. Considering the total emissions of the countries, the emission from food production comes third, next only to US and China at the first and the second slot. The food wastage alone accounts for around 3.6 times of the water consumption of the US. At last, from an economic perspective, the wastage accounts for around one trillion dollars' worth, which is higher than the GDP of Switzerland and Netherlands.

Another interesting aspect that we have developed in improving the agricultural yield is the use of antibiotics. While I was writing this article, I came across the wondrous fable of how Alexander Fleming saved the life of Lord Randolph Churchill's son, Winston Churchill, when he had pneumonia during his childhood, with his discovery of Penicillin. Since the story was touching and humane, I did a little bit of search on how antibiotics evolved. Since the penicillin was discovered and became the most effective life-saving drug in the world, conquering such dreaded diseases, such as tuberculosis, gangrene, syphilis, pneumonia, gonorrhoea, diphtheria, and scarlet fever, mankind has discovered around 100 varieties of antibiotics. It is estimated that penicillin alone has saved at least 200 million lives since its first use as a medicine in 1942, and its discovery was ranked as the most important discovery of the millennium by Swedish magazines in 2000. The discovery, not only led to a cure for bacterial infections that were once deadly, but it also led a huge interest in finding new antibiotics.

Out of my curiosity, I started to check about the size of the market of antibiotics. I was amazed at the growth that the market has seen over the period from 1928 when penicillin was discovered till date, a growth to an approximate size of US$45 billion. Furthermore, the interesting fact to note was that around 50 per cent of such antibiotics are used in the cultivation of crops and rearing of livestock—not on humans for which they were intended for. Technically, antibiotics are the drugs given for treatment of bacterial infection. Even though they are not effective against viruses, they can even target fungi and parasites. Have you ever wondered how antibiotics kill invading bacteria leaving human cells? They work by attacking things that bacterial cells have different from human cells such as the structure of cell membranes and the machinery they use to build the proteins.

Different groups of antibiotics have different ways of attack. Some attack the cell walls, some block the protein building, and some breaks the strands of the DNA building process. When one consumes antibiotics, it enters the blood stream, killing bacteria indiscriminately—that may include both malicious and friendly. But how do these affect the animals in which we use these antibiotics? By the way, would you be surprised to know that these antibiotics are not used to fight diseases that spread among animals, but to increase their weight and ensuring higher meat output? These antibiotics increase the growth rate of pigs and chicken resulting in far greater usage of such products in swine and poultry. This usage has a long history. With the worldwide population explosion, livestock industry in US had to rear larger quantities of animals over a short period of time to meet new consumer demands. When the density of the animals reared increased, it subsequently increased the threat of diseases, therefore requiring a greater disease control of these animals. This need was catalysed by the publication of Cyanamid magazine on the research establishing the practise of adding antibiotics to animal feed increased the growth rate of livestock in 1950s, accelerated the use of antibiotics, which currently accounts to 15–17 million pounds of antibiotics for subtherapeutic usage (for the purpose of feeding) in the United States alone each year.

The biggest controversy with administering antibiotics that are used to treat humans to the animals resulted in developing drug resistant variants of bacteria in such animals. It is an interesting paradox that despite various studies published, warning the development of drug resistance of certain bacterial strains due to the indiscriminate use of antibiotics for subtherapeutic purposes, the usage is still unchecked in most developed nations!

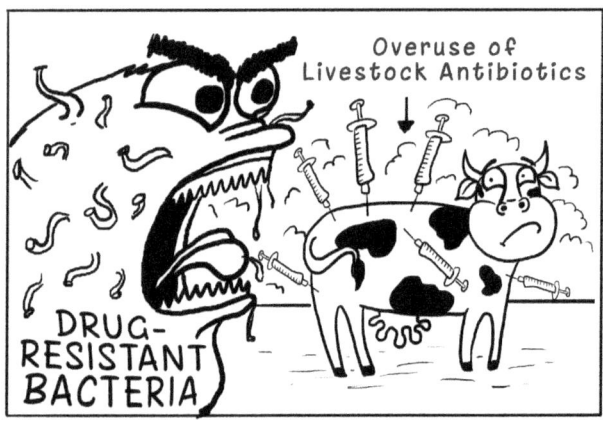

On one hand, we have an impending problem of growing population and an even bigger problem of feeding them; and on the other hand, there are challenges faced by the scientists to provide safe and sustainable sources of tasty and nutritious food. As the population increases to nine billion by 2050, humans will be putting strain on almost all natural resources such as agricultural land, water, forest, fishery, and biodiversity resources. To balance the efficiency of production, the only way forward would be to develop or migrate to a food culture that would have a high food conversion rate (lower resources for higher quantity of nutrition). To give a perspective, crickets need six times less feed than cattle, four times less than sheep, and twice less than pigs and broiler chickens to produce the same amount of protein. In absolute numbers, crickets would require only two kilograms of food for every one kilogram of body weight gain. This statistics reveals that such insects emit lesser greenhouse gases and ammonia, helping the effort to cool the planet. In addition, the rearing of such edible insects is a low-tech and low capital involvement process. This would be one of the best options for the poorest countries and societies to participate in eradicating poverty. Are they really worth consuming? According to FAO, for two billion people, over 1,900 species of insects form part of their traditional diet. So as of now, we have one-fourth of the world population already entomophagous (having one form of insect in their diet).

The top varieties that are being consumed globally are beetles that account for around 31 per cent, caterpillars around 18 per cent, and the bees and wasps forming around 13 per cent. The research by FAO mentions that the nutritional value of an edible insect depends on the group of species, metamorphic stage, the habitat, and its diet. For example, the mealworms contains unsaturated omega 3 and 6 acids, proteins, vitamins, and minerals that are comparable to fish. I believe this information was already available for the authors of the Bible. Hence, entomophagy (consumption of insect for meals) was allowed in the Bible, making it not a taboo for every next person on the planet. (Refer Leviticus 11:20–23).

If the insects are really worth consuming, then why not we try them if they are not even a spiritual taboo? I would definitely give it a definite yes. It would be further interesting when our kids get us bugs or worms for a protein-rich diet. But are we ready to accept such a meal instead of beef and chicken? If we consider the alternative to eat these 'cold-blooded bugs', a change synonymous to the shift of our generation from incandescent bulbs to LEDs, the future food platter would be more sustainable and nutritious. The process of manufacturing bugs consumes minimum energy and a lot less land, considering the factors of production for other sources of food.

Another alternative that can be seen in future could be vertical farming. Even though the concept was used a long time back by the Native Americans, the term was coined by the American geologist, Gilbert Ellis Bailey, in 1915. This concept integrates the agriculture into architecture. It may solve the need to have an agricultural area equal in size to roughly half of South America to feed the population expected by 2050. In 1999, Dr Dickson Despommier's estimated that a single thirty-storey vertical farm could feed over 50,000 people, which would translate to around 160 similar structures providing food for all of New York year-round without being at the mercy of seasonal swings. The technology can be even refined with the hydroponics. This is a method of growing plants using mineral nutrient solutions without soil. Even though this technique was demonstrated by Francis Bacon, it was William Frederick Gericke of the University of California at Berkeley who promoted this technique as an efficient crop production technique. With pest problems reduced and nutrients constantly fed to the roots, productivity in hydroponics is extremely high.

When the technology becomes more efficient, the current industrial and technology districts may alter its size and shape, and suit itself to semi-agricultural factories producing year-round produce through indoor farming aided by such technologies. Even though we haven't been able to perfect the formula for baby milk since last 200 years, we would be forced to perfect the formula for food in the pill if that could partly solve the instant food problem for the rich.

What would be the economic impact of these technologies? The current consumption of meat is over 200 pounds per person per year in the US (In India, it is just around six pounds). It is estimated that around 200 gallons of water are consumed in the process of making a single pound of beef, and around half of it is consumed in the process of making poultry. If there is a shift of the non-vegans in developed economies to any of the alternate sources of protein in the short term, the transition will have a huge impact on the economics of natural production of food. According to Marco Springmann at the University of Oxford, if people follow the current trends of food consumption instead of following more plant-based or balanced diet, it could cost the global economy up to US$1.6 trillion by 2050. This estimate is based on the 'social cost of carbon,' an estimate that values the future damages in healthcare and climate-related events caused by each additional tonne of carbon emissions.

Springmann also estimated, using a less intuitive measure called 'value of a statistical life', that the savings from not eating meat would be around US$20 trillion to US$30 trillion worldwide by 2050. For this cost to be saved, world's population would need to reduce red meat consumption by 56 per cent, increase fruit and vegetable consumption by 25 per cent, and consume 15 per cent fewer calories overall. This would be a serious benefit for the countries, such as the US, where on an average, a person eats 322 quarter pound meat burgers a year. Each burger would need 400 gallons of water to produce. Taking this consumption for one year is equivalent to the amount of water used an average American residence uses. This would be the motivation for the new technologies to emerge in developing sustainable and gastronomical delights over the next few decades as the promise of the Japanese restaurant menu. I wish this would happen soon.

The food was the original social network that transformed the group of humans to societies. May future generations consider options such as having bugs instead of beef, or a vegan burger from pea proteins made by 'Beyond Meat', and a deep-learned computer-controlled vertical agriculture containment that reduce water consumption usage—maybe through hydroponics, and thus reducing greenhouse gases. On the production side, we could have artificial-intelligence-powered crop production by identifying areas to cultivate optimised for climate and end user distribution, deciding the suitable fertilisers, and selective watering. These fields open up tremendous opportunities for the new technologies to mushroom, but I wouldn't be impressed with technology until I can download food online. Hail the kids who would decide that for us!!

WHAT IS SO COMMON BETWEEN A COMMUNITY OF ANTS AND A BITCOIN?

It was a lazy Sunday of last summer; it was scorching hot outside. I slept over till ten in the morning. The moment the air conditioner was turned off, I couldn't lie as the temperature inside room shot up to thirty-two degrees Celsius. Not so happy to wake up, being lethargic, I was yawning and sitting in the bed. I was a little surprised to see that neither my kids nor my wife was there with me on the bed. I thought they must have woken up early and must be busy with the breakfast. I was wrong.

Last Friday, I had visited one of my friend's home. Though he was my long-time friend, I never knew that he had moved out of his routine job and started a hobby shop. From the college times, I knew he had some weird hobbies. He was the only person whom I knew could catch a live scorpion with an empty bottle. So when I went last week to his home, I had taken my kids too. Although I expected uncommon creatures in his collection, I never expected to find a live ant colony, a formicarium, in his living room. My kids were so excited to see that. Even though he was not a myrmecologist, a person who studies ant behaviour, he could give a lot of insights to me and my kids on how they behaved as a group and as an individual.

I asked my friend to explain how he started this colony of ants. According to him, a single queen ant is the origin of the nest. Picking the queen ant from the wild during mating season, and dropping it in an adoptable environment, is the best bet to make a colony. Ants have a specific period of the year called 'nuptial flights', a few weeks within the year when mating occurs. The only ants involved in this mating event are young queen ants and male ants. They are born in the nest, and wait all year until it's time for nuptial flight mating. These ants are special as they are born with wings. All the ants we commonly see walking around above ground are all barren females. During the nuptial flight, the young winged queens and males fly into the air. They mate while flying or upon landing, and then finally drop to the ground a few hours later. The males die after mating. Breeding with the young queens during nuptial flight is their only purpose in the ant world.

Mated females break off their wings, and begin searching for a new location to begin their own colonies, as they won't be accepted in their own colonies. This is the time when we take the queen to build the colony. Then as couple of months advance, the queen gives birth to a small colony of a few workers. Then it takes about a year of focused care to get them to a mature colony of 100 or more ants. My kids and I were quite impressed about these creatures by listening to his lecture.

So when I asked my wife, while sipping my morning coffee, she mentioned that my kids have gone crazy about these ants are running around our house to capture the queen ants. A little curious, I too started to read on how ants colonize a locality and connect socially. The first formicarium was built by French polymath, Charles Janet, to reduce a three-dimensional ant nest to two-dimensions between two panes of glass. The true guests in here are ants. Ants evolved around 110 and 130 million years ago from wasps to form over 22,000 species. In terms of sheer numbers, they outnumber humans by leaps and bounds. Even though they are so tiny, scientists estimate there are at least 1.5 million ants on the planet for every human being, each with an average weight of 0.003 grams. To put in perspective, the total biomass (mass of living biological organisms in a given area) of the ants is roughly equal to the total biomass of the humans—100 million tonnes, even larger than that of blue whales.

A little bit on the physiology of ants, an ant has only around 250,000 brain cells. Unlike us, ants rarely use sound or sight to communicate. They use scented chemicals called pheromones that are produced by Dufour's glands found at the posterior end of their body. These chemicals are used to communicate with their family. The interesting aspect is that an ant never disagrees with what it has to do. It follows its own 'programmed' rules and signals in the forms of pheromones, vibrations, and touch. There are about ten to twenty different pheromones, each representing a 'chemical word' that the entire colony understands. This chemical communication system has been perfected through evolution that makes these creatures build complex nests, and even create rudimentary agriculture and public health systems, and thus an excellent social community.

To a give a little better perspective of what they could do, ants started farming much before human started to settle and do agriculture. Fungus farming ants began their agricultural ventures about seventy million years before humans thought to raise their own crops. It would be humiliating for us to know that they even used sophisticated horticultural techniques to enhance their crop yields using secreted chemicals to inhibit the mold growth. In addition, they have vast social networks that can stretch thousands of miles resulting supercolonies.

On the other side, at the age of 5, a human baby has over 1,000 trillion neural connections. Over time, it refines itself and transforms the number of neural connections to just over 100 trillion, just one-tenth of the original quantum. The transformation of these neural connections is the basis of human intelligence, which has evolved not just though chemical communications but through the senses and feelings that are generated in human brains as electrical pulses.

As humans, where are we headed now? Intelligence has helped us to develop social and economic networks over the period of human evolution. Even though the food was the primary motivator during its formative ages, later when the networks evolved, it got transformed into knowledge and information. On a lighter note, this can be compared to the changes in the primary drive of females in selecting their counterparts over last few generations. In the primitive society, the parameter for selecting the mate was his physical appearance that guaranteed the supply of food, but in civilised societies, this criterion has tilted more towards economic stability and intelligence. You can never see the future. It could be gauged on the social networks the companion is part of!

The modern history of social networking can be traced from the time of billboards—the bulletin board system from the early twentieth century. These boards were maintained by hobbyists to communicate with a central system where they could reserve airline tickets, access financial data from standard and poor's database, download files or games (many times including pirated software), and post messages to other users. The bulletin boards such as Fidget and CompuServe gained interest during the '80s. With the emergence of the Internet in '90s, the linked bulletin boards started to act as a medium of communication between the mainframe computers.

The true precursor for the social networking came with the emergence of AOL. There were times when AOL was the Internet, and its members created communities, listing pertinent details about them. But when the real Internet emerged, Yahoos and the

Amazons were born, and the race to keep a PC in every American home started. Soon, an era of social networking sites came through. Classmates.com was born to connect with the alumni; asianavenue.com and blackplanet.com were born to connect Asian and Hispanic communities. Then came friendster.com, which was in line with sixdegrees.com that was formed after a comment by Kevin Bacon that no person is separated by more than six degrees from another.

The era of serious business networks started with LinkedIn in 2003, which currently boasts around 300 million users. Even though the Myspace was a predecessor to Facebook by having adult crowd and content they liked, Facebook, with its sheer size, humbled every other social networking sites. I don't think the thumbs up (Facebook's ubiquitous 'like' button) has been used so effectively after the times of Romans. Based on this platform, the new specific applications are being created such as for public images, Instagram, for the private sharing of images sharing, Snapchat, for augmented reality, Foursquare, and for location-based matchmaking, Tinder. We have been discussing about social platforms and their evolutions, but we cannot talk about economics of networks without discussing the evolution of the money and its role in modern society. I guess the key difference between the ants and humans in terms of the economics of social connections was the value humans have derived from the power of networking. Even though the 'formicarium' could evolve and derive the benefits of being a collective society, it could not consider other aspects of 'economics' just because it couldn't have money associated to it (assuming that ants could think and derive value just as the way in which we could do!). The modern social networks cover all aspects of society including economics, culture, and even technology.

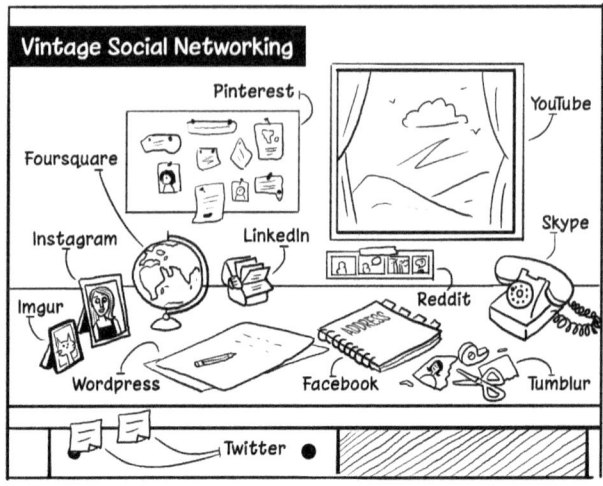

The plethora of the social benefits that mankind gained over the centuries can be attributed to the human interactions that happened as part of interacting economic systems, especially the systems of global trade. From the process of barter that was driven more by the exchange of produce to the current digital currency driven by Internet, human interactions has changed the way in which humans think. The excavations found at Ebla, one of the trading cities from the third millennium BC, give us a glimpse of how the trade evolved, and how important was it for ancient civilisations. The global trade began with waterborne traffic through the rivers of civilisation—the Nile, the Tigris and Euphrates, the Indus, and the Yellow River.

According to Aristotle, money came into existence when the inhabitants of one country became more dependent on those of another, and when they imported what they needed and exported what they had too much. Around 15,000 BC, mankind started to use obsidian, a naturally occurring volcanic glass formed as an extrusive igneous rock as a token of exchange. From 9,000 BCE, cattle were used as currency, and there are records that substantiate that the Romans and the Greeks had been using sheep and oxen for payments. When trade between the civilisations started, the medium of exchange evolved to softer commodities that could be transported easily such as spices, silk, and textiles. Then it slowly transformed into metals where humans had even an island named after the copper (Cyprus, in Latin, gives copper its name, *cyprium*, related to cuprum). It was the Mesopotamians who developed the concept of true commodity money around 3,000 BC. They used shekel as the unit of money to define both specific weight of barley and equivalent amounts of materials such as silver, bronze, and copper (even the modern currency, the pound, in its original form was a measure of one pound of silver). More than the need, it was a necessity for the early generations.

Early references to the use of money are illustrated in the Book of Genesis in the Bible when Abraham purchased the Cave of Machpelah, a burial plot. With the code of Hammurabi, the oldest and the best-preserved law code, the requirements of the society grew from just the barter to engaging into contracts, resource lending, and complex businesses leading to the better usage and circulation of commodity money. The first manufactured coins seem to have taken place separately in India and China around 700 BC with the start of the coin age. Soon, gold and silver were used as the common form of money later throughout history. Even though metal coins had a value for themselves, stability came to the currency market when national banks started guaranteeing a specific rate for these coins. This was a major step in the evolution of money, since this step initiated the change of a coin being a unit of weight to a unit of account guaranteed by a central authority. The commodity value, a unit of value, changed to specie value. This marked the beginning of modern economy where the value of money was not directly related to the value of the commodity with which it was made of. Today, a few zeros that we see in an account defines the power of money that we control.

Even though the story of evolution of money is interesting, a few interesting aspects of the old currency exchange standards still exists in some different corners of the world. In certain areas, such as New South Wales, people, even today, use rum as a medium of exchange. In prisons where conventional money is prohibited, it is quite common for cigarettes to take on a monetary quality. The essence is that man, at all times, had specific exchange instruments for the specific needs. Today, although much of the money used by individuals in their everyday transactions is in the form of currency notes and coins, we keep a fair amount of money in the form of numbers at banks. This money exists only as debit and credit entries in bank records, which is a notional amount that gives a feeling of security. In future, we could see the complete disappearance of coins and banknotes, as cowrie shells did in the early civilisation when the commodity money arrived. The transition of the mode of storage of money from the physical commodities to digits has been gradual, but quite impactful. Let's dig a little bit deeper to understand how big is the entire financial industry has transitioned into the digital space that use the power of networks.

According to Cap Gemini, the global non-cash transaction volume has reached over 400 billion with an annual growth rate of around 10 per cent. Even though the growth had a low base, the plastic transactions saw a growth of 80 per cent alone in Asia. This gives an indication of how currency is going to look in the next decade. More than the physical money, the power of money is going to be depicted by the digits in the bank account, or possibly just cash on the Internet, the digital currency or cryptocurrency. One thing that comes to mind when someone mentions digital currency is bitcoin. For most people, bitcoin is only an online social and digital currency they have come across in a few news articles recently. But did bitcoin appear out of the blue? Was bitcoin a novel idea of Satoshi Nakamoto?

The answer is no. Theoretically, bitcoin is an old wine in a new bottle, an old idea with a new flavour. If you think about money, it is just an accounting system that says who owes what to whom. In such a scenario, you need someone who is a trusted third party who keeps tab on the ownership—in today's world, the central banks. This is where the distributed ledger technology of bitcoin has evolved.

Bitcoin is just a money accounting system. It just records the value, and does it digitally in an open ledger, a consensus-based system; hence, no fees, no intermediary, and no corruption. Just a matter of coincidence, it just started in a few weeks after the complete US financial system collapsed with the bankruptcy of Lehman Brothers. The best element of bitcoin is that it is not controlled by any central company or a person. Beauty of bitcoin is it is easily transferable and anonymous, and by 2140, there is going to be twenty-one million bitcoins. Simply put the gap that the emergence of bitcoin is addressing the need of a third-party intermediary such as PayPal, Western Union, Visa, or any bank to send the money, and a central monetary authority to monitor the ownership who, in turn, takes around 5–10 USD for transaction. In case of bitcoin, there is no need of either, and in addition, similar to the equivalence of gold, there is only a definite amount of bitcoin, a characteristic that will protect the bitcoin from the inflationary pressure.

Why I am saying bitcoin will protect us from inflation if used properly? Let us look into some interesting snippets of history. There is a small country in Africa named Zimbabwe. It was one of the original British colonies with the name, Rhodesia—named after Cecil Rhodes who obtained a mining concession from a local king. After independence in 1965, Britain imposed sanctions on the country. After sorting out the internal political problems, the country was renamed Zimbabwe in 1980. The original country's currency was originally the Rhodesia pound, which was introduced at par with the British Pound Sterling. After renaming the country to Zimbabwe, they wanted to even change the currency from Rhodesian pound to Rhodesia dollars. With the conversion, a Zimbabwe dollar was valued at US$1.47. Then the tragedy struck. The farm production in Zimbabwe tumbled because of large land redistributions and drought in 1999. This resulted in a decline in the production of goods. This impacted the macroeconomy, and led to the collapse of the banking system. To make the matters worse, Zimbabwe suspended foreign debt repayments in February 2004, resulting in compulsory suspension from the IMF.

As a series of nails in the coffin, United States, the IMF, and the European Union slammed Zimbabwe with economic sanctions. This led to large budget deficits, which could only be covered by printing money. Then there was a jolly ride. The inflation rate that averaged around 10 per cent in the 1980s rose to around 20–30 between 1990 and 1997, and 50 per cent between 1998 and 2000. In 2001, the inflation rate exceeded 100 per cent, and in 2003 it was almost 600 per cent. At that point, hyperinflation kicked in. Inflation rose to 1,281 per cent in 2006, and 66,000 per cent in 2007. Suddenly, the officials declared inflation illegal. In 2008, the money supply grew by 658 billion per cent, and inflation hit an annualized 80 billion trillion percent (89,700,000,000,000,000,00

0,000) towards the end of 2008. At that point, Zimbabwe dollars were about as valuable as toilet paper.

The hyperinflation produced a dazzling array of currency denominations. The highest denomination for the first Zimbabwe dollar was 100,000 dollars. Soon, Zimbabwe issued 100 trillion-dollar note, the highest ever denomination issued for the Zimbabwe dollar. The suffering: people found it difficult to take money out of ATM machines because the ATMs couldn't handle values in billions and trillions. Customers received a 'data overflow error' and weren't able to withdraw anything. By the time the ATM machines were fixed and the ATMs allowed customers to withdraw Z$100 billion per day, that amount wasn't enough to cover the cost of a loaf of bread. If a customer wrote a check to purchase something, they were required to write the check for twice the cash price of the item to cover the impact of inflation by the time the check cleared. 'Ooh . . . that. A bingo,' as Hans Landa in *Inglourious Basterds* said. With this, people in Zimbabwe lost all trust in the government's ability to control inflation. Do we see this repeated in the economic crash of 2008?

Yes, this is precisely what happened with trust in case of the 2008 crisis, and bitcoin is trying to resolve the same. Through multiple stakeholders (in this case, the computers), the peer-to-peer trust factor is inbuilt in the system. Since the ownership of bitcoin is encrypted, you will know such encrypted identities that owned the bitcoin and the complete history of the ownership addresses of the bitcoin.

If you look at the history of economic evolution, the emergence and the impact of bitcoin has been one of the biggest socio-economic experiments that has been orchestrated in the world. On the quantity of the bitcoins that are available, there are twenty-one million coins in circulation, and best part is that each coin can be subdivided into another 100,000 parts as the circulation increases in the emerging markets. Even though it is the first decentralised peer-to-peer payment network that is powered by its users with no central authority or middlemen, from just a user perspective, it is pretty much like cash for the Internet. The technology, blockchain (a public ledger of all bitcoin transactions that have ever been executed) as we know it today, is however unique enough to change the way the whole social and financial industry works.

Before we delve into how it can transform our modern society, let us sail through the history of cryptocurrencies. There have been a few attempts before Nakamoto to bring out cryptocurrencies, but the efforts have failed because of technology, regulatory, or economic reasons.

The first attempt of its kind was e-gold by an American oncologist named Douglas Jackson. Since 1996 till 2009, the enterprise created over five million accounts. Even merchants started to accept e-gold as currency. This currency was an alternate to the Bretton Woods system in which the currency was backed by gold. The usage of the network was so huge that it became a target of cybercriminals, and their continued attacks led to the mistrust on the platform. Slowly, the platform made its own death. In 1998, a global settlement system, another form of digital currency, came into existence. Based in Moscow, Web Money offered peer-to-peer payment solutions, merchant services, online billing and payment, and Internet-trading platforms by aiding its users to set up wallets in various currencies. Having over thirty-one million users, the platform exists, even today, supporting currencies from USD to even bitcoins.

Web Money was the pioneer of the concept of online wallet and was based on the concept of underwriters who participated in the system from various countries and jurisdictions. They stored valuables of various legal nature to guarantee the transactions that were done through the network. Later, entrant to this market was the Liberty Reserve in 2006. Since it created a centralised anonymous money transfer business, it became one of the favourites of money laundering and illegal activities.

The main concern with Liberty Reserve was that the platform lacked the account verification, which made it vulnerable to money launderers. When Perfect Money fixed this problem in 2007, customers from Liberty Reserve flooded to Perfect Money after the former was shut down by regulators. The talk of the time is the newest entrant into this market—the Bitcoin, introduced in 2008.

When Satoshi Nakamura, in 2008, introduced the concept of the blockchain technology and the corresponding distributive network, it was the personification of Sigmund Freud's comment about the origin of civilisation, 'The first human who hurled an insult instead of a stone was the founder of civilisation.' Here is the era of superintelligent blockchains—intelligence built by the intelligent to make decisions. This technology is currently a baby born with unlimited possibilities to transform the way the business is done.

The refinement of this intelligence will be a unicorn in the financial technology space. Unlike other digital currencies, as we have seen in the past, bitcoin has an advantage in the form of its decentralised nature, which leaves the whole platform in charge of a much larger community of the miners (the technical term for the guarantors) than an individual or a corporation. Since the bitcoin protocol is an open source concept, it would prevent anyone from having a monopoly over the whole system. The security and transparency associated with bitcoin has gained the trust of tech geeks all over the world. Even the central banks have launched digital currency to replace their paper currency.

In 2012, Royal Canadian Mint created a digital currency by name MintChip, the first endeavour by a developed economic institution. MintChip was a smart card that holds electronic value, and can transfer money securely from one chip to another. Like bitcoin, MintChip does not need personal identification; and unlike Bitcoin, it is backed by a physical currency—the Canadian dollar. Even though it was sold at the beginning of 2016 to Toronto-based nanoPay, similar endeavours can be expected from the regulators. By the end of 2015, Ecuador has set up Sistema de Dinero Electrónico (electronic money system) to allow citizens to set up accounts and do transaction on cryptocurrency. Now, with the introduction of this electronic money system, it will be the first country to have state-run electronic payment system. According to the economist, Diego Martinez, a delegate of the president of the Republic to the Board of Regulation and Monetary and Financial Policy, the cost of saving that the country has apportioned through digital currency is around three million dollars. This comes from the huge cost that would be saved by moving to electronic mode of money instead of exchanging the deteriorated old notes for new dollar. How this transition will impact the dollar and the rest of the world is yet to be seen.

Even though I am not a programmer and do not know how to code, there was a spark of excitement when I first heard about blockchain technology, distributive ledger, and bitcoin four years back. These technologies are synonymous to open source payment platforms, unlike the closely guarded platforms of the banks and payment institutions. The evolution of bitcoin is similar to that of the Internet. There were initial comments about the Internet that it was of no good other than to distribute porn, but the transformation that the Internet brought to our lives is incomparable to any previous technologies.

So how does this technology work? I will give you an analogy for the blockchain. Assume that you have a cake to be distributed among friends. In the old school, you give it to a friend, and he may take a fair chunk of cake to get it distributed evenly. In the blockchain concept, you hire butlers. The butlers do not charge a chunk cake, and since they are wearing the butler's gloves, if they eat, you can see that on their gloves. The butler is rewarded if s/he distributes the cake in a fair manner, and it is just a small piece of cake, unlike what your friend would take. Such butlers are called miners, a very funny word, though, in the blockchain terminology. On the serious side, when the payers initiate a bitcoin payment through a third-party wallet software, the transaction is broadcasted on the global bitcoin network. At a specific interval, special computers (miners) collect a few hundred transactions and combine them into a block, reaching a consensus on how this block of transactions should look like. These miners are rewarded for providing the computer power as a stake in the smooth functioning currency of bitcoin enterprise. Once the consensus is reached, they transmit the blockchain to the entire network recording the transactions in the latest block, which will be seen in the wallet of the payee as confirmation.

What would be the impact of this technology on global payments? The largest market share in processing payment transactions is around eighteen billion dollars transactions a day by the credit card company, VISA (with around 25,000 transactions per second). It charges on an average around 3 per cent for such transactions. Bitcoin (with around seven transactions per second), in its infancy, is processing around half-a-billion-dollar-transactions daily with transaction cost less than 1 per cent.

On the global remittances platform, the intermediaries, such as banks and fund transfer agencies such as the Western Union, move around 800 billion dollars through the payment network. They, in fact, charge around 10 per cent commission. The revolution of blockchain would trim such fat commissions to less than 1 per cent. According to Goldman Sachs, blockchain technologies would bring a net savings of over a whopping 200 billion dollars a year in global payment commissions.

So what would be the future of blockchains? Firstly, the technology would be a death blow for the inefficiencies in payment systems and will bring down the transaction cost on cross-border payment systems. The venture funding of BitPesa, a Nairobi-based remittance start-up and earth port that allow real-time cross-border bank payments, are a few examples of the acceptance of the blockchain technologies. Secondly, since the ledger is transparent and trusted, the third-party cost currently enjoyed by the banks in the valuation and securitisation of the assets, will go off. The open ledgers may allow the global corporations to publish financial statements runtime rather than quarterly, which would wipe off the lion's share of commercial and investment operations of the global banks. On the flip side, its association with Silk Road (online black market and the first modern darknet market, best known as a platform for selling illegal drugs) has left some people to suspect the concept of bitcoin. Considering these pros and cons, how can we draw the picture of the economic impact of blockchain? With the acceptance by central banks, these cryptographically secured currencies will become the pulse of the world trade as the green back is now.

We can possibly give an analogy of Napster, the pioneer of the peer-to-peer file-sharing service that went online in 1999. The Napster provided free access to millions of music tracks and inspired peer-to-peer file-sharing sites. Despite its dubious origins, it inspired the development of startups such as Skype (for telephony) and Spotify (for music streaming). In the same way, bitcoin has inspired the evolution of peer-to-peer financial platforms on lending, insurance, and investment opportunities. According to McKinsey, with the emergence of the common public ledger by bitcoins, the need for reconciling each transaction with a counter party in the financial industry will disappear, saving over twenty billion dollars for banks and financial institutions by 2022.

The success and trust in the idea of blockchain are seen with the formation of blockchain start-up by twenty-five banks in the US, called R3 CEV, to develop common standards for the use of blockchain in the financial industry. If one examines this technology critically, trust machine that mints these bitcoins will take away the business of the institutions that are involved in such business as banks, clearing houses, and government authorities that are deemed sufficiently trustworthy to handle transactions. There are 2.5 billion adults in the world who do not have access to bank accounts. The distributed ledger technology has the capacity to bring those people into financial system. They can have a bank in their pocket. This could open up commerce to a lot of people much more than we could ever imagine.

These social networks, without the intermediary, form the fabric of personal, financial, and economic behaviours. This is the fundamental framework of how the rules of pheromones work with the ants and the blockchains work for humans in the current digital age. Right from the basic needs that form the basis of relationships among friends and relatives to influencing decisions made by many of the companies regarding with whom and how they conduct their business, the social and financial networks continue to play a key role. By 2016, it is estimated that the size of the social economy (i.e., over 80–90 per cent of the Internet economy) is expected to be around 4.3 trillion dollars in the G20 countries with three billion users globally. According to Bill Gates, 'We always overestimate the change that will occur in the next two years and underestimate the change that will occur in the next ten.'

To give a perspective of the explosive growth of computing power, if we take that analogy, the first Intel 80386 chip, introduced five decades earlier, had around 275,000 transistors and the current core i7 has 2^{13} times more transistors. An interesting illustration has been provided by Ray Kurzweil in his book, *The Age of Spiritual Machines*. There was a rich ruler who agreed to reward an enterprising subject by starting with one grain on the first chess square, and subsequently increasing the number of grains with a multiple of two for every next square for the next sixty-three squares. With the thirty-two square, the ruler owed the subject around 100,000 kilograms, and with the sixty-fourth square, the ruler would own 461 billion metric tonnes over 600 times than the world rice production on 2015. Thus, the tremendous value that humans are going to derive from the explosion of Internet, and thus digital social networks, can never be underestimated.

How does this impact the way in which we live? How many of us do product research online and purchase offline? As per the research conducted by BCG, the products worth more than 1.3 trillion dollars has been purchased globally in 2010 in such a manner. By 2020, it is estimated that there will be fifty billion devices connected to each other over the Internet. According to McKinsey, the Internet of Things or IoT will have a total potential economic impact of US$3.9 trillion to US$11.1 trillion a year by 2025, accounting for around 11 per cent of the world economy, making it Internet of everything. Imagine the value of transaction that is expected to be flowing through the global networks over the next few decades with the elimination of the trusted intermediaries and global payment systems. Social network is expected to become much larger and more powerful like the last thirty-two squares when the pile would challenge the magnitude of Mount Everest.

Anyway, these may sound too complex to understand and too futuristic, but the future is rushing towards us. In addition to the ocean of opportunities, risks do exist. Without proper regulatory policies and technology framework, this explosive growth could be disastrous. But scalable, automated, and instantaneous nature of these superintelligent blockchains would change the world as we see it today. The openness to change and the acceptance of disruptive technologies would craft a brave, new world—a world of simplicity and innovation. For those willing to think big, embrace change, move quickly, and organise differently, there are tremendous opportunities to reap rewards of the creative destruction of the social and economic networks.

I reach home, tired after a hectic day at the office. The door opens at my presence. Hot tea is served on the table. Just in the oven, I smell the sweet aroma of freshly baked chocolate chip cookies. I walk up to my wardrobe that assists me to change my attire. Soft jazz plays as I step into the Jacuzzi that knows my favourite scent. Soft, but intense water drops with my mood to give me a hot shower. Undisturbed by the jazz, key market updates play in a binaural tone. As I get out of Jacuzzi, the ambient temperature changes to adjust to my body temperature. The oven picks up the temperature, and hot food heated is served on the table. TV gets switched on to my preferred channel. The aroma in the room is still intact. Lights in the room adjust to my liking.

This is not a utopian *Star War's* movie. This could be a normal household that would come in the next few decades. If this can happen based on the current technology, my imagination is limited to think what's beyond in the social and economic world—beyond in the social and economic world.

4

THE CURIOUS CASE OF SMART CONTRACTS

Anytime when my wife and I fight, first thing that I would say to her is that I will get a divorce. Last time, we had a grave fight. I wanted her to learn driving, and she was trying hard but could not. I felt that she was not trying hard enough. For no reason, I lost my temper and told her that she is not taking any responsibility, and I am fed up living with her, since she keeps on accumulating the responsibilities of any logistics upon me under the assumption that I would take care.

'Enough,' I shouted.

'I too agree. I am going home.' She became a crouching tiger and retaliated.

She dressed up, packed up her dresses, and got into the car. We were not speaking. I was driving quite fast, and the air was quite cold; we never talked much. I was quite rude that I kept on thinking how I could divorce her. She appeared sad. When we reached home, I was still full of temper. I ferociously told her that I am going to divorce her. She was broke. I saw her running into the house in despair. On the way back, I kept on thinking what is the fundamental of marriage, and why do we have a divorce too. I decided to read about the origins of marriage, why there is a need for a divorce if there are concerns in the marriage, and how normally it is solved through divorce if there is no emotional way out.

The union of a man and a woman, recognised by authority or ceremony, is as old as human civilisation itself, and marriage of some kind or form is found in virtually every society. The marriage was borne of ancient societies as a need to provide safe environment to breed, handle the granting of property rights, and protect bloodlines. Even though the marriage is a contract between two people, and with the society to ensure these fundamental rights, sometimes marriage took an emotional angle too.

The angle it gave is much about love and desire, as it guarantees social and economic stability. In this concept of roundness, the engagement ring, a custom dating back to the Ancient Rome, is believed to represent eternity and everlasting union. It was also once believed that a vein or nerve ran directly from the 'ring' finger of the left hand to the heart, giving the store a love a reminder of the wedding. The striking attraction for me was the concept of contract that enticed and preserved the wealth of generations. Rather than focus on the divorce part, I focused on the fundamentals of contract, as my head cooled off from the temper. One day, I got a call from her.

'Hello?'

I understood she could not speak. I thought of breaking the ice. With the break of ice, my anger also melted off. We had a long chat, as usual, and put my conditions, and we decided to forgive each other as usual. This was my part in one of usual cacophonies of married life. Is it just the emotional connect that held our marriage? It is not. It was the strength of holy matrimony as believed by Christians. Nutshell it is the strength of the contract that my wife and I had entered into at the time of the marriage.

But after this incident, I started to think about the impact of a contract in our daily lives. Right from the money/currencies that we use for daily purchases to the job we do, and from place we stay to the utilities that we consume, all are based on one single understanding of a contract in the modern way of life. As per the definition of contract, it is a written or spoken agreement, especially one concerning employment, sales, or tenancy that is intended to be enforceable by law. The underlying need for any human for

7d8640747 87324680

---

a sustainable living is the urge for making the money through various activities. In a country like India where there is a spurt for digitalisation, over 86 per cent of the money that's in circulation is in paper. So what is paper money? It is just a piece of paper that the users respect as a primary contract with the central bank. On an Indian currency, the governor of the Reserve Bank of India promises to pay the bearer the denomination of the currency. How does this line give the underlying purchasing power to the paper?

A banknote or a paper currency is a type of negotiable instrument known as a promissory note, made by a bank, payable to the bearer on demand. It is the promise of the third party to fulfil the commitment that gives the piece of paper the power of value. The idea of using a lightweight substance as evidence of a promise to pay a bearer on demand originated in China during the Han Dynasty in 118 BC. For a surprise, this contract was made in leather and was backed by the power of the dynasty. The first paper currency was also developed in China in the form of privately issued bills of credit or exchange notes, and the history says that they have been using the currency for more than 500 years before the practise began to catch on in Europe in the seventeenth century.

It took another couple of centuries for paper money to spread to the rest of the world. The funny part is that in the meantime, the Chinese too got into a recession—a fairly advanced financial crisis. The causes attributed by the historians were the lack of regulations to control the production of paper notes and an economist who could think about the economic impact of non-discretionary printing and circulation of currency, prompting a severe inflation across China.

The westerners at that time were busy into expanding their reach and knowing the uncharted territories of the world. The explorers and the adventurers were always fascinated to find the end of the world as we knew then. When the man believed that the world was flat, he always wanted to see what was on the other side of the horizon. The invention that aided him to explore and discover new territories was the magnetic compass. Before the compass was invented, man oriented himself to the path followed by the sun, stars, and the landmarks. When the man started to notice the characteristic of the magnetite in the fifth century BC, he identified that a freely floating magnet will always point in the north-south direction.

As a precursor to the compass, the Chinese developed the south-pointing carriage in which the pointing arm always pointed to the south without fail. The Chinese had various funny models in place that made use of this fundamental principle such as wooden fish floating on water with magnetite in its stomach and a rotatable wooden tortoise attached to a bamboo pole. They were the first group to use the magnetite for navigation, and this heralded a new urea for trade in the twelfth and thirteenth century. Without the knowledge of the compass, Columbus would not have dared to venture into the uncharted water for the discovery of India, and Magellan wouldn't have circumnavigated the world. Anyway, the west connected with the east for good.

Once the concept of currency came to the Europeans, they too did make currency as a tender of exchange, but there was slight difference. Since gold were almost accepted universally in the sixteenth century, the goldsmids or goldsmiths controlled the supply and holding of Gold. These goldsmith bankers began to accept deposits in the trade centres of the world such as Venice. As a token of the possession, they gave receipts. Even though they used to keep token of receipt, they had a system of notes to record what deposits they held. They signed such notes to attest their value so that their clients could keep. Over time, they had created, by convention, an informal market, and these notes operated as virtual money, since the currency was backed with corresponding gold with the bankers or the goldsmiths. This change was the beginning of an ever-evolving lending and payment system in the world. Such framework made the loans and transfer funds possible.

Progressively, they also started giving receipts for cash, which promised that the corresponding gold coins were deposited with them. These receipts came to be known as 'running cash notes'. They were made out in the name of the depositor and promised to pay him on demand, and hence were started to be called as promissory notes. But such notes could be exchanged only with the person who owned the gold with the goldsmiths. Since the logistics and the trade increased, the concept of the bearer slowly crept in to the system. This meant that not just the person who owned the gold could get it exchanged; even the person who was carrying the note could enjoy the value of gold. This allowed the circulation of such notes in a limited way among the community of traders. This guild of goldsmiths, the Goldsmith Company, had existed in various forms since the fourteenth century and continues even today as the worshipful company of goldsmith in the city of London.

The spurt in the economic activity through the trade and commerce forced the thinkers to invent an instrument that would count the large quantity and value of the goods easily. It was neither easy to carry nor safe to use the gold equivalents of wealth. The primitive systems of accounting started with the Egyptians and the Babylonians who arranged the goods in a group of ten after the number of fingers in the hand, while the Roman counted the same in a group of five. Following the mathematicians, the traders traced a grid of longitudinal and cross lines in the sand for counting and assessing the value. Each little counting stone had a value assigned to it. The longitudinal columns represented the decimal system in rising sequence from right to left. Nine stones lay in each column, each being added from the bottom upwards in the course of counting. When all the stones of a column were in the upper part, a new group of ten would be marked by the first stone in the next column, and the nine stones were moved back to the starting point. The upper side was divided up crosswise into sects in which the traders noted the value of the particular item. Soon, the sand was replaced with wood and metal and name for this calculating device emerged as abacus. Through the trade routes, this found its way to the Greek and the Romans. The latest computer and the calculators have not replaced the abacus completely. The same is being used in China (suapan), Japan (soroban), India and Eastern Europe (stschoty).

To know the economic evolution, one must understand how England evolved as an economic power. The story of central banking goes back to the seventeenth century to the founding of the first institution recognised as a central bank, the Swedish Riksbank. Established in 1668 as a joint stock bank, it was chartered to lend the government funds and to act as a clearing house for commerce. Even though the British developed the concept of central bank, it was formed not as a clearing house, but as a private institution that could raise debt for the monarch.

The story starts with the glorious revolution of 1688, which resulted in the deposition of James II and the accession of his daughter, Mary II, and her husband, William III, prince of Orange and stadholder of the Netherlands. More than the political impact of the revolution developed a concept of the central bank, not because for the need for financial stability, but because of the mess created by the monarchy after the expensive wars such as Battle of the Boyne in1690, and war with France in 1689. The bank was founded by Royal Charter in 1694, and William Patterson build a proposal to finance the government debt by private subscription of individual shareholders. According to him, a bank has to be built for the convenience and security of great payments, and to better to facilitate the circulation of money. He also laid the foundations of having a sound credit. The benefits to the shareholders would be that in return for the capital invested that would finance the government debt, their company would be incorporated by Royal Charter and become the only limited-liability entity allowed to issue bank notes and trade in bonds and relend against the government debt. These powers enabled the bank to have a monopoly at that point in time, although within a few years, however, would that be challenged by the founding of the ill-fated South Seas Company, which would compete with the Bank of England. But for the moment in just twelve days, the full £1.2m subscription was raised; and in current value terms, that sum would be worth much more today. Half was promised to be used to rebuild the navy and start reassertion of Britain's empire protected by a recovered naval power.

This was a profound moment in economic history, and significantly influenced markets around the world as well. This was the first time the power of a third party was acknowledged in the financial contract. The Bank of England bought heavily in to government stock and issued notes on the security and ownership of that debt, while also accepting private deposits. This was the start of the process of managing debt as an intangible asset represented by, say, a banker's note or bond that had in itself no intrinsic value (useless paper) unless realised in a tangible asset of value such as gold. In essence, a banker's note would still hold a value and represent an obligation to pay on demand if required under certain agreed conditions in gold the equivalent value, but of course the material or paper that it was written on was not where the value was realised, but in the equivalent gold value it represented.

The banknote evolved and was modelled on the receipts and notes used by the goldsmiths. The concept of the National Debt and Paper (note) based money came into being, at the same time, as the bank opened for business. The government needed to spend more than it was earning as income from taxation. I believe all should be familiar with this concept?

Anyway, by 1708, Bank of England was granted the monopoly to issue bank notes; and in 1717, Sir Isaac Newton, the master of the royal mint, established a new mint ratio between silver and gold that had the effect of driving silver out of circulation and putting Britain on a gold standard.

The gold standard, which prevailed until 1914, meant that each country defined its currency in terms of a fixed weight of gold. Central banks held large gold reserves to ensure that their notes could be converted into gold, as was required by their charters. When their reserves declined because of a balance of payments deficit or adverse domestic circumstances, they would raise their discount rates (the interest rates at which they would lend money to the other banks). Doing so would raise interest rates more generally, which, in turn, attracted foreign investment, thereby bringing more gold into the country.

A political cartoon from the 1940s critizes
Pres. Roosevelt's decision to take
the U.S. off the gold standard.

Central banks adhered to the gold standard's rule of maintaining gold convertibility above all other considerations. Gold convertibility served as the economy's nominal anchor. That is, the amount of money banks could supply was constrained by the value of the gold they held in reserve, and this, in turn, determined the prevailing price level. And because the price level was tied to a known commodity whose long-run value was determined by market forces, expectations about the future price level were tied to it as well. In a sense, early central banks were strongly committed to price stability. They did not worry too much about one of the modern goals of central banking—the stability of the real economy—because they were constrained by their obligation to adhere to the gold standard. Hence, for all central banks were the lenders' last resort at the time of financial distress such as bad harvests, defaults by railroads, or scramble for liquidity by wars.

In parallel, the US also had two central banks in the early nineteenth century: the Bank of the United States (1791–1811) and a second Bank of the United States (1816–1836). Both were set up on the model of the Bank of England. But unlike the British, Americans bore a deep-seated distrust of any concentration of financial power in general, and of central banks in particular, so that in each case, the charters were not renewed. There followed an eighty-year period characterised by considerable financial instability. Between 1836 and the onset of the Civil War—a period known as the free banking era—states allowed virtual free entry into banking with minimal regulation. Throughout the period, banks failed frequently, and several banking panics occurred. The payments system was notoriously inefficient, with thousands of dissimilar-looking state banknotes and counterfeits in circulation. In response, the government created the national banking system during the Civil War. While the system improved the efficiency of the payments system by providing a uniform currency based on national banknotes, it still provided no lender of last resort, and the era was rife with severe banking panics unlike the British heritage.

Anyway, the emergence of the currency created the need of contracts in our everyday life. Unlike the earlier currencies backed by the gold, the value of today's currency is determined by a collective fictional story based on contracts. The fictional quality of money is inherent in the very idea of money. It is just a warrant that can be executed wherever required to satisfy your need or identify a value. We derive value because we have collectively decided that it should carry some value through the exchange rates set-up. Money that is promised by any central bank is not an objective in itself. It is the collective fictional story, which begins with the central bank and the people.

Over the past two decades, the concept of the money as a storehouse of value and medium of exchange has transformed the monetary contracts of currency into digital money that changes into 1 and 0s on computers. The numbers are underwritten by the large financial institutions such as multinational banks. They are the gatekeepers of today's money and not the central banks. Soon, the guarantee of such institutions will have more power than the central banks. With the innovation coming through in term, the payments and the store of money, the central challenges of the central banks are yet to come in. Today, instead of physical money, more transactions are done on digital or programmable money.

The evolution of today's digital money can be compared to the history of automobiles. The first car was slow and hard to understand. People could not understand why the engines are better than the horses. Similar to this, the transition of paper money to digital money is like the transition of horse and carriage to IC engine. Initially, these clunky machineries appear to not go anywhere and seems to be slower than horse. But once the engine is refined, there have been businesses developed based on the engines. The same way, once these new technologies evolve, even though scary, we have to become the slaves for algorithms. This may be new role of new central banks, to decouple the need of large trusted institutions to democratise money that can be beyond borders and accessible to everyone. So tomorrow, we may have cash, card, a few numbers, or even a car-sized stone—the yap of Micronesia as our currency of exchange.

But then, how will our contracts be honoured? By definition of contract, it is a voluntary arrangement between two or more parties that is enforceable at law as a binding legal agreement. In the New Age, contracts will evolve to computer protocols that facilitate, verify, or enforce the negotiation or performance. That's what has been happening in the case of distributed technology of blockchain—the bitcoin (there are lot of variant of the same bitcoin) and Ethereum.

Since we have discussed on the fundamentals of blockchain and bitcoins, we will discuss a little bit on the technical of the Ethereum. It is an open source public blockchain-based distributed computing platform, featuring smart contract functionality that, I believe, there is lot of potential in the eras to come. The virtual machine of Ethereum can execute peer-to-peer contracts using a token called ether. The concept was initially proposed in late 2013 by Vitalik Buterin, a cryptocurrency researcher and programmer. Smart contract is just a phrase used to describe computer code that can facilitate the exchange of money, content, property, shares, or anything of value as a contract. When run on the blockchain platform, a smart contract becomes a self-operating computer program that automatically executes when specific conditions are met. Since these smart contracts run on the blockchain, they can be programmed to perform without any possibility of breaking the privacy, censorship, downtime, fraud, or any third-party interference. Unlike bitcoin, these smart contracts use the blockchain as a platform on which the code can be executed autonomously. The smart contracts can thus interact intelligently with other contracts, make decisions, store data, and act as a storehouse of value to others. This means developers can build thousands of different applications that go way beyond anything we have seen before.

Let us take an example a parent's need to transfer a fixed amount to his child on every birthday. The contract made on this platform can automatically transfer money to their child every birthday without breaking the privacy of both dad and kid. Contracts are specified by their creators. In this case, the dad, but the execution is done on the Ethereum network on a payment processing program. These contracts will execute, and the program will be self-destructed if the dad has kept it as a one-time transfer. If not, the process will get triggered as decided by the frequency set by the dad. As far as the regulators are concerned, they can use the blockchain to understand the activity in the market, maintaining the privacy of the individual actor's positions.

Ethereum is the second most popular cryptocurrency. As of now, Ethereum accounts only one-tenth of the market capitalisation. The control of the Ethereum is done by Decentralized Autonomous Organisation, which will code the decision-making tools. So how does this platform transform the way in which the world works?

Any services that are centralised can be decentralised using Ethereum. This includes all the intermediary services that exist across hundreds of different industries. From financial services, such as loans and credit cards provided by banks, to intermediary services such as property registries, voting systems, market and regulatory compliance, and much more. Ethereum enables developers to build and deploy decentralised applications. Since these decentralised applications are made up of code that runs on a blockchain network, they are not controlled by any individual or central entity, limiting the involvement of the intermediaries, which reduces the chance of single point failure or a hack.

In this context, it is worth mentioning the local currency of New York, the Ithaca Hour, which is the oldest and largest local currency system in the United States that is still operating. The primary function of the Ithaca Hours system is to promote local economic development. One Ithaca Hour is valued at US$10, and is generally recommended to be used as payment for one hour's work, although the rate is negotiable. Even though the currency is not backed by green back and cannot be freely converted to national currency, the concept of this currency puts forth the idea that economic interactions should be based on harmony rather than on more Hobbesian forms of competition. Thus, one underlying principle of the local currency movement is to create fair trade with a minimum conflict or exploitation of either people or natural resources.

With the strong sense of deglobalisation in US, Europe, and even Asia, I believe such local currency economies will start soon. On the economics of Ithaca Hours, several million dollars value of HOURS have been traded since its inception in 1991, among thousands of residents and over 500 area businesses, including medical centres, the public library, local farmers, movie theatres, restaurants, healers, plumbers, carpenters, electricians, landlords, etc. On the spending patterns, the businesses that receive Hours must spend them on local goods and services, thus, building a network of inter-supporting local businesses. While non-local businesses are welcome to accept Hours, those businesses need to spend them on local goods and services to be economically sustainable.

To promote the concept, the association made also interest-free loans of Ithaca Hours to local businesses, and grants to local non-profit organisations, which boosted local economic development. A similar effort was done by the officials of Berkshire County.

They created a currency by name Berkshares with 100 Berkshares equivalent to US$95. Such local currencies will foster the money circulation within the community, and make money a means rather than an end in itself. The local currencies receive discounts at local stores; hence, the customers and the merchants have incentive to purchase from nearby suppliers for cheap prices. Such transactions incentivize producers to produce more. The local economic grows, and money stays in the community.

We are now living in the era of deglobalisation and the sharing economy. The same concept of local currency will still prevail, and the Ethereum can connect both consumers and businesses to turn their assets into income. In such case, to boost the local economies, nations will move to even small currency associations where the currencies may not be accepted nationwide, but will be honoured in a specific area. If we look at the economics of sharing economy, according to PWC, it has created seventeen different billion-dollar companies with 60,000 employees. The sector, per se, has received close to US$15 billion in funding, and its global yearly revenue is projected to reach US$335 billion by 2025. On the demographics of the people, who uses this economy, include the age range of 25–45 with an income range of 25,000–100,000 USD, which is the crowd that would use the emerging technology. As per the survey, around 44 per cent of the population of US is familiar with the sharing economy.

I believe, very soon, Airbnb and Uber will be fully automated, and small business owners will prefer to rent private workspaces and private cars on demand rather than commit to complex leases or purchase a car. Once the Ethereum platform kicks in, the intermediaries, such as Airbnb, may vanish or evolve as platforms based on distributed ledgers where the owners in a sharing economy become both consumers and producers. The millennials' philosophy is fast becoming 'if you can rent it, why own it?'

Sixty-six per cent of the world is willing to share or rent their personal assets for financial gain, and that figure is as high as 94 per cent in China. Crowd-sharing apps are geared to increase efficiency in a user's life, ensuring that needs are easily met. On the other side, these apps can be problematic. They eat away established markets and businesses. Since such apps need not pay expensive business licences, pay wages to professional staff, and conform to regulations, they are able to offer prices that are much lower than the market. If such the community could leverage the Ethereum platforms to earn an income without losing revenue to a third-party intermediaries, it would even change the current sharing economy. Even the banks can be part of this revolution. They can be the facilitators of the business. Assume a retail store needs a loan of US$100,000. The bank can fund half of it, and the balance can be funded by the customers who would be given vouchers, which give the customer additional value. In such a case, the US$50,000 can be obtained by selling US$120 vouchers at US$100. Here, the bank underwrites lesser risk, the store gets funded by its customers, and the customers get value on investment. I believe once we merge the concept of Ithaca Hours and the sharing economy, the concept of money itself may disappear with the appearance of the smart contracts, which would take over the world, since everything can be defined under a smart contract as a storehouse of value—the idea for the existence of money as we see today. Now, I have a good reason to bargain with my wife. You never know we may be towards the last leg of the generation that took pride in owning something. Who knows it may include the subtle subjects of marriage and money.

THE GUNS OF GOOGLE

It was a cold rainy morning of July. I could hear the rain pitter-patter on our rooftop. I was lying cosy in my bed to avoid getting completely woken up. 'Ringgg!' It was my mobile that I forgot to put on silent mode the previous night. Being a little lethargic, enjoying the cold, and humid morning, I just rolled over the bed with my pillow. The phone just slipped from the tabletop and fell to the carpet. I didn't bother to check who was ringing, but the ringing stopped. My joints and the neck were in pain from the tedious Krav Maga session the previous day. Before I realised the pain and the phone call, I suddenly felt bullets going left and right. It was just as if I did the Normandy landing. I am quite sure that you remember the scene from *Saving Private Ryan* when the spiralling bullets are all over the water, and you can see the corpses all over. The cold chill was suddenly felt by my body. Suddenly, I got hit on the hand, and my hand was terribly frozen with pain. I just fell into the water and was getting drowned. There was a ring in the water. Oh, it was just a dream and the ring was from my friend again.

Being a naval officer, my friend, Cyril, is always on call of duty. I never expected a call from him unless he wanted something urgently. I took the call. 'Joe, I need a help.'

'Yes, sir, at your service.'

'We have a competition here. It is to submit a book review, and I need your help in getting one entry to participate.' As quick as he were already, 'I will give you a call in the evening to discuss further. But you finalise a book that would be of your interest.' Saying this, he cut the phone. By that call, he transferred the onus of selecting the book and writing about the book to me, which, I felt, was the hardest task on a cool Sunday morning.

Without much of options, I started to ponder in the bed itself on a book that would make sense for him and will have an impact as a naval officer. As a gleam of enlightenment, *The Art of War* that is attributed to the ancient Chinese Military strategist, Sun Tzu, came to my mind—the military treatise dating from the fifth century BC.

I brushed up the content that I had read a few years back. I could relate some of the current political and technology strategies that are getting reflected in the words of Sun Tzu. Anyway, I could relate many decisive naval strategies, especially in the planned battles in line with that of Sun Tzu. One of the interested quotes that I was interested and that I stressed in the article was on the relevance of deception in the achievement of concentration at a decisive point. He stressed that the art is to practise deception and manipulate the enemy so that he will fight on his terms. Those who are skilled in enticing the enemy with something he is certain to take, and with lures of ostensible profit, they wait for him in strength to retaliate. The perfect application was seen on the naval engagement by Queen Elizabeth I with Spanish Armada in 1588. Off the coast of Gravelines, France, Spain's so-called Invincible Armada was defeated by the English Naval Force under the command of Lord Charles Howard and Sir Francis Drake.

In this engagement, around two hundred English vessels met the great Spanish Armada in the English Channel. The English crafts were widely dispersed at sea and technically nimbler with well-furnished guns. The might of the English fleet was disguised with the spread out strategy of the English. In a naval battle, it is easier for the enemy's fleet to avoid battle at sea than it is for an army to do so on land. Hence, if the opponent realises they might of the opposing fleet, it is more likely that the weaker opponent will avoid the battle. Only through dispersing, or rather pretending to disperse its fleet, can the stronger navy lure the enemy into battle. This was precisely what the English Navy did. They did not concentrate on the war front. This made them easy to conceal its whereabouts and movements. This strategy that encapsulated the iconic Sun Tzu's approach that calls for the need to keep one's own dispositions shapeless in order to avoid disclosing one's intentions forced the engagement of the Armada with the English. Once in battle, the English could break up the Armada formations, and could attack its great vessels one by one. The English managed to drive the Spanish Armada out to sea, marking the beginning of the era of 'the empire on which the sun never sets'. This decisive defeat of the invincible Armada made England a world-class power, and introduced effective long-range weapons into naval warfare for the first time, ending the era of boarding and close-quarter fighting.

With the theory of war, management of soldiers, and deception over my usual cold coffee, the book review for my friend was done. But this unexpected critical analysis of the book made me think the technology strategy adopted by the technology, Leviathans, of our era. Leviathan is term coined for the sea monster in the Tanakh or the Old Testament. It is a word that is used contextually for the sea monster. You may be thinking what it has to do in an era of the technologies that emerge even before the predecessor makes its presence. Though the term was coinfed out by the seafarers, the term came to my attention after reading the book written by Thomas Hobbs. His argument for the necessity of absolute sovereignty emerged in the politically unstable years after the Civil Wars of England, which underlined the existence of unseen Leviathan for a stable society to prevail, and equal justice for the equal imposition of taxes.

Yesterday morning, I was surprised to see a buzz on my phone. I thought I had kept a reminder and just tried to switch it off. It didn't go off. I was surprised to understand that it was an alert regarding my upcoming flight that had been pre-poned by forty-five minutes. I was little curious. I checked my mailbox, and I had accidentally deleted the mail that had come from the booking agency. I called up the agency to confirm and it was confirmed. Wow! I appreciated the effort Google has done for me. I felt happy and relieved.

On the flight, I started to think about the technology that we are depending on. The phone has been so intelligent to know exactly what we do, where we are, and more than that, why we are where we are? Isn't that intrusion of personal life knowingly or unknowingly, or can I term it as an information slavery?

Humanity have come a long way from the discovery of the electromagnetic telegraph was by Baron Schilling in Russia in 1832, which was the baby step in the field of communications through the power of electricity to the Internet of Things and moving ahead to Internet of Thoughts. Soon, the wireless transmission of the Morse code, 'What hath God wrought?' from Washington, D.C. to

Baltimore was a milestone that is still respected in the history of communication. Slowly, these communication devices became a prominent part of common man's life. But it was only in 1990 when John Romkey created the first Internet device—a classic toaster that can be turned on and off over the Internet through a TCP/IP protocol—changed the way in which man could communicate with the devices. Soon, a group of students from Carnegie Mellon University made a networked Coke machine—the very first Internet appliances that inspired the evolution of modified versions that allowed machines to serve people. Trojan Room Coffee Pot created in the Cambridge University also followed the queue in which the appliance could be controlled over the Internet.

But the term Internet of Things was coined by Kevin Ashton in a presentation that he made at P&G in 1999, linking the new idea of RFID to P&G's supply chain to the then-red-hot topic of the Internet. Soon, LG, the consumer electronics giant, came out with the plans on first Internet refrigerator. The new dimension of the IoT was defined in 2005 when UN's International Telecommunications Union (ITU) published its first report on the topic. Conceptually, the IoT implies physical objects being able to utilise the Internet backbone to communicate data about their condition, position, or other attributes. The report predicted that by 2020, Internet of Things will create a plethora of innovative applications and services, which will enhance quality of life and reduce inequalities, while providing new revenue opportunities for a host of enterprising businesses. The journey post 2008 was remarkable. The IPSO alliance, an alliance to promote the use of Internet Protocol (IP) in networks of smart objects, and to enable the Internet of Things was born, which currently has members over fifty companies including Google. In the same year, National Intelligence Council, US came out with a report that listed Internet of Things as one of the six disruptive civil technologies with potential impacts on US interests out to 2025.

So how will the IoT change the life of a common man? It is estimated that by 2020, there will be a staggering seventy-five billion connections within the vast network of approximately twenty-five billion smartphones, appliances, manufacturing equipment, and wearables—referred to as Internet of Things or IoT. There are a few sectors that would have big impact with the arrival of IoT. These numbers strongly indicate the influence that machine-to-machine (M2M) connectivity is going to have on our society, culture, and business. According to Gartner, the economic benefit estimated from this business is around US$2 trillion. Early movers in this field are the commercial real estate and the insurance providers. According to Gartner, smart commercial buildings and smart homes will be the highest users of IoT going forward by which the technology can reduce energy use, repair, and maintenance, and administrative costs at least by 30 per cent. The biggest breakthrough would be when the continuous monitoring and predictive capability of IoT will pre-empt a repair or maintenance issue by enabling a building manager to take appropriate corrective action before tenants even notice a problem.

One day, in not-too-distant future, when a building manager and tenant sit down to negotiate over the terms of a new lease—the building itself not the manager—will hold most of the cards in the negotiation. The building itself will have the complete idea about how much a tenant uses a building's facilities, and how has been the usage of the tenant of such facilities in his earlier leases. The building be a constellation of data that surrounds every aspect of its operation, and it can negotiate itself rather than humans negotiate for them. In addition, homes, office buildings, warehouses, and factories have sensors installed to detect temperature, smoke, toxic fumes, mold, earthquake motion, or other hazardous conditions. With two-way communication, these IoT devices can also provide predictive alerts on potentially dangerous conditions in the near future. This arrangement will work for both insurer and the insure, and the role of the real estate intermediary or the broker in the common man terms will be gone again.

IoT is not only changing the real estate segment but also it has a huge impact on the real money matters too. Couple of weeks back, I had been looking on a question in which there was a critical reasoning in which it asked for how insurance would be different for same car based on the usage pattern. The answer hinted the usage of driving analytics to identify the pattern of driving of the car. Now, let's look at how it is done?

The auto insurance industry nowadays uses telematics. Through the GPS and various sensors connected to the new-generation cars, a driver's behaviour and the health of the car is continuously monitored directly while the person drives, and this information is transmitted to an insurance company. The telematics devices measure a number of parameters, which are of interest to insurance agencies such as kilometres driven by the driver, which time of day, the number of minutes the vehicle is being used as recorded by a vehicle-independent module transmitting data via cellphone or RF technology, location of the vehicle, acceleration, breaking, etc. The company then assesses the risk of that driver having an accident, and charges insurance premiums accordingly.

While there are rewards for good driving, it also acts as a deterrent for rash driving, and hence promoting safe driving through providing incentives for doing so. It also helps drivers to reduce the accidents frequency, improve tracking to recover stolen vehicles, easier claims settlement, among others. The acronym they mention for this technology is UBI (Usage Based Insurance) or PHYD (Pay How You Drive) or Mile-Based Auto Insurance. So how do they assess the risk and the premium in the UBI? All-state and progressive along with the startups such as Metromile have been the pioneers with the UBI platforms. They claim to reduce the unfair treatment to low-mileage drivers who overpay to subsidise high-mileage drivers. They charge a flat fee, and based on the miles driven, they charge a cost equivalent to usage and these companies that specialise in collecting location data.

The same way the user's health monitored by wearables, devices that can be worn by a consumer and often include tracking information related to health and fitness are changing the health and term insurance too. The users are getting rewarded for sharing their movement data. All of these devices are part of the so-called quantified-self movement, which is about blending each aspect of your life with technology that continuously gathers and crunches data. Ultimately, all these gadgets for the part of Internet of Things, an all-encompassing phrase that describes interconnected digital gadgets that log, report, and control data from your body and across the planet.

Do we have any ethics in the management of these personal information? Pretty much sure that everyone is aware of the Holocaust during World War II. Nazi physicians had subjected Jews to a murderous regime of medical research. The Holocaust resulted in the systematic annihilation of six million Jews by Nazis. Out of which 1.5 million murdered were children. After World War II, in October 1946, the Nuremberg Medical Trial began, lasting until August of 1947. Twenty-tree German physicians and scientists were accused of performing vile and potentially lethal medical experiments on concentration camps inmates and other living human subjects between 1933 and 1945. After these trials, the Nuremberg Code, a set of ethical guidelines for human experimentation, came to existence, which is governing human medical research. Similar to the healthcare experimentation ethics that has been guaranteed as part of the Nuremberg Code, another set of code will soon form the basis for technology privacy.

The decline of mobile hardware, as we had seen with Motorola and Nokia, and the emergence of data and IoT giants, such as Google and Apple IOS, may transform the political landscape too.

JOSEPH ANTONY PULIKKOTTIL

The news of Apple steam rolling FBI to protect the data privacy laws is still a controversial topic to discuss. But I believe that we have come to an era in which the private enterprises could stand against, even the Uncle Sam. But are we acknowledging that there is no data privacy for us when we indiscriminately use our Facebook and WhatsApp?

It may look for a better future too. Currently, we have an intermediary that take care of our security at the expense of taxes—the government. What is the role of government in everyday life? According to the constitution of United States, the government exists to ensure a perfect union, to establish justice, to ensure domestic peace, to provide common defence, to promote general welfare, and secure the liberty. Let us look these roles from a technology parlance. Considering the information the technology company holds about the individual, I would not be surprised the religion of technology behemoths transforms itself to countries. All roles that the constitution tries to ensure, through the government, would be enabled by such technology behemoths through an integrated approach. I look forward to an era in which the borders vanish and world political powers will be dislodged with the emergence of super data powers. The unequal taxation and the borders will go off-limits, and the world would shift to a data constitution and, indirectly, a data citizenship. You never know it, maybe soon that you enlist with super data powers and pay tax so that your civic and social rights are guaranteed!

But how it will work? Let us list out what these social Leviathans know about me. For example, Google has a simple tool called Google Analytics. It is possibly the best brainchild of Google. This takes the complete stocks of pages that one visit in his/her net presence. Right from our erogenous zones to the plans of our future, today, we express our needs to the Internet. This is what builds this Leviathan, giving access to the information such as how many times you have visited a website/a location place (in

78

case you have geo-tagging is in place), how long did you stay in that web site/location, etc. Even if you do not do it consciously, do you cherish the moments when Google Maps came for your rescue when you were lost, or when it recommended you to take an alternate route when you were stuck in highway traffic? If yes, then that will answer the question if right with you. To know what you believe Google knows, you just need to search the history of activity. This captures the complete history of your searches, YouTube videos that you watch, the maps that you have searched, the news and the advertisements you clicked in the past, and the latest addition of Google Now, an intelligent personal assistant developed by Google that uses voice search and commands.

How is Google managing the show? Whenever one uses Google, it gives consent to the company to share data across a wide variety of embedded services in millions of third-party websites using Adsense and Analytics. The collusion of Google and the Uncle Sam is quite evident with the comment that in December 2009, after privacy concerns were raised, Google's CEO, Eric Schmidt, stated, 'If you have something that you don't want anyone to know, maybe you shouldn't be doing it in the first place. If you really need that kind of privacy, the reality is that search engines—including Google—do retain this information for some time, and it's important. For example, that we are all subject in the United States to the Patriot Act, and it is possible that all that information could be made available to the authorities.'

Even at the Techonomy Conference in 2010, there was another fair comment he predicted that 'true transparency and no anonymity' is the way forward for the Internet. 'In a world of asynchronous threats, it is too dangerous for there not to be some way to identify you. We need a name service for people. Governments will demand it.' He also said that, 'If I look at enough of your messaging and your location and use artificial intelligence, we can predict where you are going to go. Show us fourteen photos of yourself, and we can identify who you are. You think you don't have fourteen photos of yourself on the Internet? You've got Facebook photos!,' Now you don't need to bother how famous one would be in the Internet.

There is another key item of interest. It is the cookies and how the companies track the user behaviour. Unlike the chocolate chip cookies, these are small files, which are stored on a computer. These files are designed to hold a modest amount of data specific to a particular client, website, and the information the user had looked at, and can be accessed either by the web server or the client computer.

There are two types of cookies: first party and third party. Third-party cookies are those set not by the site you visit, but by some other advertising site. Most browsers enable third-party cookies by default. Some, like Google's Android browser, don't even give you the choice. The more effective method that has evolved on the principle of cookie is the advertiser ID. These are similar to third-party cookies, but make third-party cookies less effective as a privacy mechanism, and place the control of privacy into the hands of the company controlling these advertising ID—in this case, Google, Apple, and Microsoft.

Since Google's 95 per cent of the revenue is dependent on advertising, with the usage of these advertising IDs, Google become more powerful and can dictate what to be shown to its users on its discretion. The best part is that no one in this power struggle is advocating for consumers' rights. No one seems to be really bothered to help users to make informed decisions about how they're being tracked and what information is being maintained on them. Every computer or smartphone is set up so that multiple companies can and will track your activities across large numbers of websites that they don't own. The truth is that cookies are really just one head of the emerging hydra, and not even the most insidious one. Most web pages are not atomic entities, but crazy quilts of scripts and images from up to dozens of different sites. A typical web article will have ads provided by several networks, each on different domains, a comments system provided by another third party, Twitter and Facebook integration, and analytics code to track site visits. So most any commercial website loops you into this byzantine network of ad networks, ad exchanges, data exchanges, and trading desks.

Research by Know Privacy, a portal on web privacy, data collection, and information sharing indicated that more than 88 per cent of websites inform Google of your visit for advertising, analytics, or some other purpose. So once you are on the net, better be sure that you are doing the right thing. In Eric Schmidt words, 'If you have something that you don't want anyone to know, maybe you shouldn't be doing it in the first place.' Isn't this the strictly a materialist view of the world that Hobbes' thought where human beings are physically sophisticated machines of whose functions and activities can be described and explained in purely mechanistic terms.

Am I getting to the society of Hobbesian philosophical system, which had its origins in the fear, possibly this time not as absolute sovereign, but as a technology sovereign? Hope not.

6

WHERE ARE WE EVOLVING TO?

The world of science has always intrigued me from the day on which I started to think. The fascination of life and death and the path in between them has always been thought-provoking for me. This fascination has driven me to such an extent to deliver such a humble representation of discovering the economics of outlier scientific concepts and dimensions that changed the way the man lives.

I don't believe that world has changed significantly from the times of Newton to the modern times of Stephen Hawking. My belief in the economics comes right from the times when human being started from the discovery of the nature to satisfy his hunger. From the ancient times in which he hunted for food using his primitive tools and organised hunting in groups. From the ancient tools that he used in the Stone Age to the New Age inventions in the information age exemplifies his achievements, and each of these inventions or discoveries provide a whole bunch of economic sense. In this dialogue, I would try to do a qualitative analysis of various leaps of novel ideas of science that have contributed to a huge economic value for the mankind.

We cannot treat any leap of science just in its value in science but also in its uniqueness, age in which the human race had made the progress, the value the invention creates in the current society or in the society in which the invention was made, and an economic sense of the inventions. From the Stone Age times, when the human beings started using the numbers for all practical purposes of living till the latest era of human genome, the transformation of science has been through the various interpretation and observations of scientific data based on the numerals. The development of the complex number system from the naming of the cardinal numbers by the Sumerians and Babylonians, and the usage of numeral zero in the Arabic system by the Indians, paved the way for the new dimension of scientific thinking and analysis. The revolutionary changes that have been brought since the same have contributed to the change of the mankind ever since. In brief, the world is, today, can be described in a binary sequence. From the thoughts that we capture, the lines that are being typed by me on the computer, to the likes of our tastes that we capture through the Facebook is nothing but combinations of 1 and 0.

So what actually changed the way in which we think? Were these binary options still existed in our ancient civilisations? Yes. But we started deciphering the world as binary only after brains started to think in a directed fashion. The famous line of Gordon Gecko, 'greed is good', must be the motivation factor for all our progress as we see today.

The fundamental urge to make more of everything than one's neighbour must have started from the basic instinct of food. When human settlements started to develop, it was not just the individual needs that came in, it was the community needs too. Here comes the need to understand the importance of hunting and war in this context. When we understand the war as a concept, the underlying principle of all the altercations that we had in the human history is rooted in greed, and the history of mankind is a story of greed, and the aspect that drove humanity was the drive that motivated the human to define territory and glorify the war, the warlords, and the veterans—an action that is still continued till date. How did the economics of war work? To see the economics of war, we need to see the wonderful aspects of war and grudge that have been used in our daily lives.

Humans fought among themselves, and with the nature to satiate this greed. In the process of satiating the greed, the evolution of the spear into a tensioned bow and an arrow was a very critical invention for the existence and satiating the fundamental needs of the mankind. The conflict or a war was waged by political entities, nations, or, earlier, city states in order to resolve political or territorial disputes, which were grounded on the economics of resources and greed. Unlike today, people considered the territory as a means to avail resources. Even though from the times when the humanity originated, there were wars. The first one in recorded history took place in Mesopotamia in 2,700 BCE between Sumer (present Iraq) under the leadership of King of Kish, Enembaragesi, and Elam (present Iran) where the latter was defeated.

There were many ancient inventions that changed the course of military history. The realisation that a pointed object could kill a fast approaching animal and equally could sew a clothing paved the way to the new civilised man. The conscious effort of precision and accuracy started when man started using the feathers on arrows to keep them in their flight level in the Bronze Age (3350–3100 BC). Once man learned the technique to domesticate the animals, he started to use them in chariots around 2,000 BC. While one man controlled the manoeuvring of the chariot, a second bowman could shoot arrows at enemy soldiers.

Have you ever wondered how Alexander the Great could come to India crossing such a hilly terrain of West Asia? He made it possible by the bridge-building. This enabled the people and goods to be transported quickly and effectively over the large rivers and deep gorges. Before the science of bridge-building, man used to search for shallow crossing in the wide rivers. The bridge-building was the start of the new stream of science—the structural engineering. Even though the Babylonians, Egyptians, and Etruscans developed the idea of structural bridges around 4,000 BC, the Romans perfected the technique, since they needed to transport the large volume of water over large distances for their ablutions.

The discovery of gunpowder and the development of firearms and cannon was one of the significant works of man that made a significant changes in the political and social arena. It was the Chinese warriors who were particularly interested in the weapons that would make the combat redundant. By the ninth century, the Chinese alchemists had made a combination of saltpetre, sulphur, and charcoal. The handgun was first introduced during the twelfth century, followed by the cannons. This reduced the physical efforts of the warriors.

Gunpowder in Europe was extensively used in the 100 Years' War from 1337–1453. But the manufacturing of the gunpowder and the cannons were banned, and as a result, Berthold Schwarz, who invented the cannon, was executed to death in 1388. Once the firearms started to be used in the fights, the traditional knights and the chivalry disappeared forever from the army.

Once the concept of territory and the nation evolved, the administration of the controlled territory became standardised. The need for the standard weights and measures became a requirement. As the trade volumes grew for the economic stability and power with the smooth function of the exchange of goods, the standards of measurements became mandatory. For length, the use of foot as a standard can be traced from even 3,200 BC. Egyptians developed the standards of weights as the coins of copper. They also developed the system of scales, especially for weighing the medicines. They saw the same as the symbol of justice, and according to their belief, in order to enter the future realm after death, one has to be weighed on the scale of honesty and justice. This belief was the precursor of having the lady justice in present-day courts. Sumerians were the first to come out with the standardised weights with the royal inscriptions to avoid manipulation by the merchants. Later in the eighteenth century, when the French took the standard of length as forty millionth of the circumference of the Earth, it marked one of the important conditions for the development of modern science and technology.

By 3,000 BC, the Nubians started to mine the copper and gold, and Egyptians started to make utensils with copper. They also accidentally discovered that the soft metal copper could be mixed with tin to make bronze that could be best suited to make weapons and tools. Bells and complete carillons were excellent examples of the art of metal-making. When the Chinese specialised in the softer applications, the Greek used the same for making weapons and armour.

The Bronze Age defined the prominence of the alloy till the harder iron replaced the alloy by 1,000 BC. When the bronze adorned the utilitarian theatre, the gold adorned the luxury theatre. Since the gold was a softer metal than the bronze, it was mostly used for making ornaments and luxury products and never in weaponry.

As we see the fast world where we talk about the speeds of fifteen times the speed of sound, have we ever thought what paved the way for the speed? Without the invention of wheel, the culture and the history of the mankind would be something completely different. The conquests and migrations of the mankind wouldn't be ever possible without a wheel. As the human race started to flourish in various parts of the world, the need for greater supplies and building materials started to emerge.

The vast appetite of the same was satisfied by the strenuous effort of the men, the oxen, and the horses. The basic idea of the wheel came accidentally when logs of wood were laid together as rollers. Around 3,000 BC, it was the Mesopotamians who cut large logs of wood into slices and attached the same to a platform so that the same can be used to transport. Since then, the evolution of wheels has never looked back. Since the wood was solid, it was too heavy and could not support the load of attaching the same to the platform. Then the concept of axle evolved, and soon the lighter wheels started to emerge as in the hub and spoke arrangement.

This arrangement led to the development of chariots that could support the rider and his armoury. It was after the full-fledged development of the road network by the Romans that the transport of goods and the travelling in wagons became common. During the Bronze Age, the woods started to get replaced by the metal, inevitably providing better comfort and load capacity.

In 1495, the artist-scientist Leonardo da Vinci wrote, 'If a man equipped himself with a dome of cloth stretched on a farm, he could jump from any height without danger.' Though he didn't try out the same, his fellow countryman, Fausto Veranzio, tried it out practically. He jumped over a ridge to try it out. In his experimental notes, he mentioned that a human can float without danger if he allows to get collected under the canopy of the parachute.

The actual flying experience by lighter air was conducted by two Frenchmen, Joseph Montgolfier and Louis Sebastian Lenormand. Montgolfier threw himself off the roof of his house with home-made parachute, while Lenormand jumped from the tree using two parachutes. For Lenormand, the purpose of the parachute was not just as a flying machine, but as a useful piece of rescue equipment in the event of a fire in a tall building. The discovery of the hot air balloon by Jean Pierre Blanchard extended the use of the parachute. In one of his flights in 1785, when his balloon was about to burst in the mid-air, he could escape in one of the parachute he had kept in the flying apparatus, saving him from a fatal fall.

By the nineteenth century, the parachuting developed as a sport and entertainment. Otto Heinicke in 1917 was the first one to develop the first automatic parachute that would open when the wearer was free in the air. He developed it in a laundry bag cushion under the seat of the pilot of the aircraft. This system was a great success, and many pilots of World War II utilised it thereafter and saved millions of lives. By the end of World War I, the parachute became mandatory in a military aircraft.

How did man know the tropospheric heights are not harmful for human being? Hot air rises, and the Chinese knew it long ago even in the Middle Ages. They lit candle beneath paper balloons and when the air became hot, the balloon rose up in the sky. Although the same was done as part of the special ritual, the principle was adopted in the hot air ballooning by the French.

The Montgolfier brothers in the eighteenth century attempted this as part of their patriotic efforts to recapture Gibraltar from British. Montgolfier brothers were owners of paper mill and supplied paper to the royal court. Once on the way back home, their attention fell on the women who was drying her wet shirt in the fire. The billowing of the shirt gave them the idea of using the hot air to make the balloon fly. Moreover, if the flight was successful, they were planning to smuggle soldiers to Gibraltar through the hot air balloons. So with the help of fabric bag, in 1782, they flew for 1,650 yards, climbing a height of 330 feet.

In June 1783, the first public demonstration took place in Lyon with the help of a balloon made of canvas and paper; they reached height of 6000 feet. When Louis XVI heard about this endeavour of the Montgolfier brothers, he was keen to explore the potential of the same. He wanted a public demonstration of the same in Paris. In September 1783, with a larger balloon, a rooster, a duck, and a sheep became the first travellers in the balloon. The demonstration of the flight inspired the French physicist, Jean Francois Pilatre de Rozier, to such a degree that he himself wanted to attempt a manned flight. He expressed his interest to the brothers, and within a month, they attempted the same. The trip lasted for twenty-five minutes, and carried Rozier over the centre of Paris into the suburbs of Gentilly. Unfortunately, Rozier lost his life in a balloon crash two years later.

The improvements on the air travel started to flow in. The French professor, Jacques Cesar Charles, who described how gases tend to expand when heated, designed the hydrogen balloon instead of hot air, which was much more effective in flight that took man to a height of 550 m above the ground. The only concern on the same was the gas was highly explosive, unlike the hot air. He followed Montgolfier brothers' naming convention and called the balloon Charlière.

But it was not yet proven that the heights of troposphere are not harmful for human. Later in 1804, it was Gay Lussac and Jean Baptiste Biot who made the first balloon ascent purely based with scientific objectives. They measured the temperature, pressure, air composition, and the magnetic field at the height of 13,100 feet, and proved that there are no significant differences between the values at the ground and at those heights, which paved the way for the aspirations to fly high.

In 1450 BC, when the Egyptians started to use the bellows in the furnaces, the world was getting slowly in smelting process by which man could increase the temperature on a metal surface by blowing pointed air flow towards the hot surface, facilitating the melting the metal. The process of making the iron, which was the fourth most abundant element on earth, to the set use was one of the greatest steps by mankind in the road to progress.

The Hittites, the Indo Germanic, were the first group of people to use iron instead of copper and bronze around 2,000 BC. The metal in the initial phase had lots of impurities, and hence was more malleable and hence was not suited for all purposes. Later, by 1,400 BC, Armenians discovered the method to harden the iron by heating it in charcoal to red-hot, and then quenching it by plunging in water. From then, iron became the material that determined the military and economic power for over 2,000 years. Romans were the first to set up their own forge in a large scale to develop weaponry for their army as the might of the empire depended upon the steeled weapons and war equipment. By the second century BC, daily life couldn't be imagined without iron.

More than these inventions on the grudge or war ground, which are used in everyday life, there are inventions that we could see in modern daily life that are outputs of the recent wars. They range from canned food, which was invented by the support of Napoleon during his European conquests to plastic surgery that was performed by Harold Gillies on a young British sailor named Walter Yeo who was wounded horribly in World War I. Even the microwave oven that was the improvement of radar, and the digital photography that was the output of the Cold War, were still the inventions of the wars. There are many things that involved with any war. On the positive outcomes, they include peace, love, money, and on the negative outcomes include debt, death, and sadness. Here, we will take a case and do an economic analysis of the cost and the outcomes of a war.

I believe we cannot take the economics of war is miniscule. If not for war, the United States of America, the world's powerful country, may not even exist. The Holocaust would've never happened, and there would be fewer countries in the world. War is something that cannot be avoided as long as humans continue to change and grow. The cycle of war will never end because it always leads to the same thing: one side winning, the other side losing; one side with pride and rewards, the other side with loss. Both sides, however, have devastating consequences that follow war. Death, debt, and poverty are some of the most major consequences that follow war. We are not here to judge whether the war is good or bad, and the emotional loss is too great that a war should be avoided in any way possible. But . . .

How does a war start? Some of them could be pride, money, land, and nationalism. Let us take a case of recent war as a reference for the common man—the Cold War between USA and USSR. The war has a motivation of pride and nationalism. It started in 1947, just at the end of World War II, and lasted until the dissolution of the Soviet Union on 26 December 1990. It was the result of continuous rivalry between these former World War II allies. The causalities of the war included the biggest cities of the world to tropical jungles of

Vietnam. On the arsenal side, the era developed nuclear submarines gliding noiselessly through the depths of the oceans to the most technologically advanced satellites in geosynchronous orbits in space. The Cold War, not just political and cultural war, waged by communists and capitalists, it was a colossal confrontation on a cultural scale never before seen in human history. This war proved the supremacy of the capitalism over communism.

The seed of such a megalomaniacal war was actually sown by Winston Churchill in his anti-communism remarks on 5 March 1946. He said, 'From Stettin in the Baltic to Trieste in the Adriatic, an 'iron curtain' has descended across the continent. Behind that line lie all the capitals of the ancient states of Central and Eastern Europe. Warsaw, Berlin, Prague, Vienna, Budapest, Belgrade, Bucharest, and Sofia, all these famous cities and the populations around them lie in what I must call the Soviet sphere. And all are subject, in one form or another, not only to Soviet influence, but to a very high, and in some cases, increasing measure of control from Moscow.'

What he said exactly reflected the attitude of Stalin in which he was conquering the complete Europe just after invading Berlin. The tit for tat response to the Stalin's effort was the Marshall plan set up by the Americans. Through the Marshall plan, the Americans propagated the capitalistic agenda across Europe, which later attracted the new-generations to get the inspiration of the American brands. The Soviets responded to this plan through Zhdanov Doctrine, unveiled in October of 1947, which promised to eliminate imperialism, and the remaining traces of fascism, and strengthen democracy. The Americans reacted to the Zhdanov Doctrine with the so-called 'Long Telegram,' written by George Kennan, deputy chief of mission in Moscow, which changed the verbal confrontation to a strategic conflict between the countries that fought side by side during WWII. Soon, they were undeclared enemies in a war that would never break out in the open, but which would last for more than fifty years. So what was the output of this war?

After the showdown in Hiroshima and Nagasaki by USA in 1949, Soviet Union developed its first atomic bomb. This development confrontation between the USA and the USSR, escalated to the nuclear level, started the nuclear club in the world, a club that though elite but viewed as a terror.

Then came the darkest and most illiberal ideas in its political and social history of America—the McCarthyism. The government, and even private enterprise, recklessly accused thousands of Americans of being communists or fellow travellers and sympathisers, and subjected them to interrogation, investigation, and sanctions. Even though this phenomenon tarnished the benevolent global reputation of the United States, the effort was extremely effective to make it the big brother of the modern economic era. The supremacy of the US was underlined with the presidency of John F. Kennedy. There were setbacks for the supremacy because of Cuban missile crisis and the Vietnam War, but still the big brother kept on watching. In parallel, another pandemonium started on space race. More than the race for peaceful and human benefit, the battlefield was for technological and ideological superiority. Soviets took the lead when they launched Sputnik 1, the world's first artificial satellite; then followed by shooting the first human, Yuri Gagarin, into space; and the first woman, Valentina Tereshkova.

Considering a few such factors, we will try to do a SWOT analysis and Porter's Five Force from the corporates to analyse the perspective of America at both current and future situations in which the America entered the war. Through this process, we will analyse the strengths and weaknesses that America had at the time of entering the war, while looking for opportunities and threats. The goal is to build on strengths as much as possible because of the decision that was taken while reducing weaknesses that could have been gone against that decision. A future threat that America had considered can be a potential weakness, while a future opportunity that they realised can be a potential strength too.

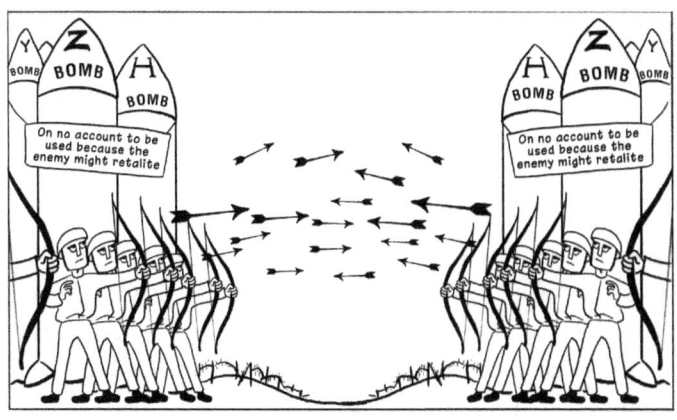

The war always defined the supremacy of a country. The economic dominance of a country is defined by the currency domination in the modern economic era. But how does America ensure that it maintains the economic supremacy? Through defence spending. I am quite sure you will not agree, but you will agree to the fact that the empire that had the strongest military always ruled the world, both economically and politically, and thus achieved the world domination. If one scrolls back through the pages of history, British defence share of government expenditures during the seventeenth, eighteenth, and nineteenth century was up to 75 per cent of GDP, never dropping below 55 per cent. The predecessors for the British were the Dutch, who had even larger numbers to boast.

If you look at the spending pattern of the US on defence, it was less than 1 per cent during the Renaissance, grew to around 12 per cent of GDP during the civil war of the 1860s, 22 per cent during World War I, and culminated to staggering 41 per cent during the WWII—the time of the universal call by Uncle Sam for the Armageddon. Even today, US Military accounts for a staggering 40 per cent of global military spending. More of a fact, US annual spending on military is higher than the next thirteen nations combined. To give you a perspective, the constitutional democracies built by the people for the people (I am not so sure about that) and of the people, as Uncle Sam says, the allies of US account for over 80 per cent of military spending of the world. Wow, that's quite a large number!

But have you really thought why this country and its allies alone are spending so much money on defence? At least for a few of us, when we speak of value, the dollar term creeps in. Why are we speaking so much about the dollar? The origin of the dollar is from Spain. Spanish called the currency as *real de a ocho,* the eight-real coin of approximately thirty-eight mm in diameter, worth eight reales, a unit of account in Spain for several centuries after the mid–fourteenth century. Since then, there were three general types of money in the colonies of British America: the coins, paper money, and commodity money. Commodity money included items such as tobacco, beaver skins, and wampum.

Even though there are over 180 currencies in the world, the cost of crude, investment made by IMF, debt of countries, and even the Big Mac Index is always measured in dollars. If we look at global forex transactions, there is a 44 per cent chance that one of the currencies in the transaction is the greenback, and hence it enjoys the status of world reserve currency. Are we reading about completely unrelated topics?

Not really. This insatiable recall/demand/a belief in dollars has handed the US Government a virtually unlimited credit card and a perfected money minting machinery. US, with a debt of about US$60 trillion, is currently the world's biggest debtor nation. Due to dollar's role at the centre of the international monetary system, US has the largest domestic debt securities market (US$30 trillion), which is more than double the size of the next largest domestic market, Japan (US$1 trillion).

The defence superiority also enables the country to forge international economic and military partnerships, a trend which points to the country's strategic clout. This is what US achieves by retaining its first rank in the defence and military spending, which otherwise would be difficult to maintain in competition for global superpower. Although China is trying hard to crack to this by making its presence felt, grand old uncle knows that military prowess and economic prosperity are not zero-sum games. Although democratic countries know that they have the potential to realise US$1.30 of extra private spending over a period of five years for each US$1.00 reduction in defence spending (study by Mercatus Centre), will our grand old uncle change its military and geopolitical strategy in emerging markets for such a silly gain? Let's wait and see how uncle tames the dragon.

But what we achieve with the war and what are the trends emerging in the demographics? Today, when I reach to a light switch in the middle of night, I do not realise that until the invention of electric light, humans had to work with the fire and oil to lighten the darkness. This enabled the human beings to lengthen the day. The man realised that the fire can be a devastating force of distraction, but when tamed, can be used for getting light, heat, and over and above cooking in the mid Pleistocene era. He began to preserve the power wherever he could encounter the same from the bush fires or from the acts of God. The heat and light of the fire has contributed significantly in developing the human brain as we experience now. A lot of inventions started happening in parallel that moulded the modern man. He started to build houses (around 10,000 BC in Jericho) to stay, and staying indoors directed him to develop calendars based on moon. He started carving the phases of moon with the bones and pointed spears. The nomadic man decided to settle and started cultivation around 8,000 BC, resulting in the development of civilisations.

The development of societies and shelters forced man to think to extend the day with the fire, and the ancient forms of lamps developed. To make the lamp portable, man made the soapstone by carving out hollows in stones. In order to intensify the light available through the lamp, the man used polished surfaces, such as mirrors, on the rear side of the lamp. The creative art that could be sold started to develop in the Mediterranean countries and in the surroundings. Workshops and household industry started to make the lamps, and thus became the first profitable branch of industry. The importance various civilisations gave for the dead increased the demand of the lamp industry. Around 4,000 BC the Mesapotamians started to make glass, and the Egyptians and Sumerians started to make copper. This paved the way of artistic works on the lamps. Soon, when the candles started to become more popular than the lamps, the prominence of the hand-made clay lamps started to fade, and the candles with shiny glass and copper works started to emerge.

By 6,000 BC, the Fertile Crescent, the land running from Syria and Palestine towards the delta of Euphrates, Tigris, and the Nile started to emerge, which is considered as the cradle of modern civilisation. The country between the rivers and the so-called Garden of Eden, Mesopotamia, the human settlements started to emerge, and man started to use the plants and suitable for the soil and the climate. Fields were set up in the fertile deltas of the rivers, and the regulated supply of water emerged. The development of early civilisation, thus, is closely connected with the invention of irrigation. This has not changed even in the modern era.

Even today, most of the developed settlements still thrive in the sides of fresh water bodies. Around 5,000 BC in the Indian subcontinent, the cultivation of rice flourished with the usage of plough. In the similar lines, the Mesopotamian civilisation also gained ground in the development of agriculture as we seen the modern times. This development forced man to work in tandem with the force of nature. He wanted to tame the forces of nature for his advantage. Around the same time, they also developed a solar calendar to establish the seasons and the passage of the year. The Egyptians developed a solar calendar in the third millennium BC so that they could foresee the flooding of Nile. Even though the efforts on agriculture emerged very early in the history of mankind, the thoughts of classification of plants into their families took a long time to develop. Ancient Bablylonian had a script to classify the garden plants when they build the hanging gardens, but it was only in the eighteenth century when the zoological and botanical gardens, in various parts of the world, people could observe the unique creatures and strange plants.

The great voyages of the sixteenth and seventeenth century also helped to shape this inquisitiveness and challenge the existing classification of the flora. The solution for this problem came from Carlus Linnaeus by classifying and naming all the plants and animals based on their genus and species name. In 1730, he published his treatise on the classification of the plants based on the characteristics of their reproductive organs, which got him the attention of the Swedish Royal Society to undertake six-month research journey. After years of work, in 1735, he published his famous work, *Systema Naturae*, in which he grouped similar species under the same genus, then orders, and then into classes. He also used this system to classify the animals too. The classification seemed simple to apply and easy to follow. Since the classification was purely based on the sexual organs, some of the classification seemed arbitrary. The need for the division based on the natural classification of the plants and animals was propounded by Immanuel Kant, which was met by the mid of nineteenth century when the biologist, Charles Darwin, appeared with the theory of evolution.

But the credit of giving each species a double Latin name with its genus and species, which enabled the scientists across the world to use the same technical terminology, has to be given to Carlus Linnaeus; hence, our name evolved as Homo sapiens.

The species that you and all other living human beings on this planet belong to is Homo sapiens. During a time of dramatic climate change 200,000 years ago, modern humans evolved in Africa. Like other early humans that were living at this time, they gathered and hunted food and evolved behaviours that helped them respond to the challenges of survival in unstable environments.

One of the fundamental property of Homo sapiens that differentiated us from rest of the genre was the sense of the community that developed among them. Sharing food is so fundamental to the human experience, the common thread of every barbecue, birthday, bar mitzvah that we take it for granted, but it is a unique and essential part of our evolutionary inheritance. In nutshell, other apes do not share the way we do.

But what are the fundamentals of the sharing economy? I believe it is trust. It's not a simple work. It is tricky, hard to explain, harder to define concept. It is crucial for so many things in our current sharing economy. As Adam Smith said, a base level of trust in society is necessary for specialisation and the economic growth that accompanies it. If we didn't trust the butcher to give us quality meat without having to inspect the cow every time—or worse, if we needed to check the saving bank account every time—the whole system would come to a screeching halt. If one were to look at any of the genre made by Immanuel Kant, I can vouch that only our species are the ones that would have trust and faith inbuilt in the character. This the fundamental building block of sharing economy. So that does it offer? On the pros, it offers flexibility, choice, and part-time income whereas on the flip side, there is no guaranteed income or hours, no standard worker protections and benefits, must pay own income taxes and social security. The speed, dynamism, and scale of the sharing economy seem to point to a substantial long-term trend.

What is at work here is a transition from traditional individual ownership of most assets towards accessibility-based economic models, which can be observed across a wide and increasing variety of markets. Two trends can be observed in the evolution of this model. Firstly, technological progress allows this new business model to spread to more and more markets, and become more and more convenient and flexible. An example of this is the Spotify, a music streaming service that provides consumers access to an estimated over thirteen million music tracks, conveniently through their smartphone, tablet, or computer. Another example is the car2Go car rental company: which provides members with flexible and local access to individual mobility through a large quantity of rental cars. Secondly, there is a shift to a peer-to-peer accessibility-based business model, centred on companies that operate through an online platform or marketplace that connects consumers, owning certain assets and skills with consumers in temporary need of them. Examples include Taskrabbit and Freelancer that allows a person to do the work without any binding to a company and Airbnb that allows to get the maximum benefit out of your assets by renting such assets.

On the finance side, there are sites such as lending club and Funding Circle that enable peer-to-peer lending, an efficient use of your money. There are several macroeconomic impact of this transition. So what are the factors driving the growth of the sharing economy? It is the trust. One side there is decreasing consumer trust in the corporate world, especially among young people, as a result of the financial and economic crisis. On the other side, the trust factor on friends, the online acquaintances have become more trustworthy than the institutions. It is just not the trust, the rising unemployment rates, and the falling of purchasing power of consumers have had a grave impact. Therefore, citizens are seeking ways to earn or save money, which is why consumers are currently more receptive to peer-to-peer business models centred on consumer needs both as a potential supplier and buyer. With the rise of services that enable the peer-to-peer economy, we have truly entered the age of the 'trust'. Traditional intermediary players are seeing their utilisation and market share decrease, and this is going into the hands of everyday people.

Furthermore, the technology required for connecting with new people and hosting an online platform have, in recent years, become more affordable. To extend this, people have become more aware of the environmental concerns and the economic waste that are generated through underutilised assets.

The younger generation is more familiar with new technologies and masters them better. This generation has also suffered most from the economic crisis, and is therefore more suspicious of established systems and open to alternative solutions. Thus, it is sensitive to the stated intention of the sharing economy, which aims to facilitate daily life by involving the end user in the production process of the service. As a result, the potential of the sharing economy is significant with annual growth exceeding 25 per cent in some sectors it could even reach 63 per cent by 2025.

From the competition, the ultimate competition the war, the world will evolve to cooperation, the ultimate cooperation and the sharing economy. From the frameworks of war to the frameworks of sharing economy is the transition and the evolution will benefit the end user. It will allow the customers and service providers to be more resourceful. Consumers can engage directly with individual service providers quickly and easily through a well-maintained platform with very low overheads compared to traditional models. People will take increasing risks because of the accountability, and the trust the social and online profiles bring. This has resulted in authentic and personalised experiences that can be enjoyed without the overt presence of a corporate brand.

This economy completely relies on reputation capital. A good reputation for providers, customers will be the key to the future development of this market. The economy will diversify from people-powered services to include assets in their own right by making use of physical items that are connected through IoT. We will discuss about this later. When the Uber driver gives you an excellent rating, it is high time that you too reciprocate that because you never know that next time you approach to a party for a loan, the rating of the driver would definitely matter for you. Is it the Leviathan watching? The trust economy is actually on trust as in sharing economy, or is it on fear from the war economy? It can be two sides of the same coin. But humans are the output of evolution, which says that the latter is true. If the history repeats, we are talking about a Leviathan that would the reason of any economy. The only question is whether it is direct or indirect, the difference is yet to be seen.

7

THE PRADA BABY, THE GOOD, THE BAD, THE UGLY?

I laid on the rolling hospital bed, was quite tensed as I was going for the first time to the operation theatre. Lot of thoughts came to my mind, as all know whether I made the right decision, not just in getting my urinary stone removed.

The thoughts of how evolved the surgery was when you could remove something from your body without any pain, and that too even without a physical incision, was an amazing thought. Before much of the thoughts on evolution came to my mind on the bed, suddenly the bed started rolling. It entered into the operation theatre. It was quite chilly. Fully steel-cladden, Dr Shetty welcomed me with his style. The anaesthesiologist was an old lady; she had her assistant. The old lady patted on my back and asked me to get up and move to the operation table. I was almost naked and half out of my mind as I was tensed so much.

The old lady asked the assistant to pick the medicine. I could see the needle; it was quite thick. Two hands, I had the needles for medicine they asked me bend and sit. By seeing the needle and the old lady, I was quite sure that it was going to be painful. I could sense the needle piercing my body coming out again and again. In fact, I was thinking it was not an injection to the spine, it was all over the spine. Every time it increased my pain. I was thinking that the spinal anaesthesia would require multiple injections. The way in which the villain in *Spiderman 2* movie had metal hands connected to his spine, I thought something of that sort was being connected to my back. Doctor was asking to bend. I did, but again, the same pain. I call Jesus. What is happening? Are they fucking around with my body? Suddenly, the doctor said, done, 'Joseph, are you okay?'

I said, 'Except for the pain of injections, I am fine.' Then I realised that the assistant of anesthesiologist was trying to get the L1 portion of my spine for injection and not as I thought. He also told me if I am interested, he can look at the monitor where you can see how the urology ureteroscopy is being done. I looked into the same. I could see in the camera what was going on. There was a tube that was going all the way some sounds as if crushing the stone. It was amazing. For a moment, I wondered how our technology has advanced. I just tried to move my legs. I could feel nothing below my hips. For some time, it was numb, and I could really understand how it feels to be out of control. After around an hour, they moved me to the intensive care unit. This was my first experience on a surgery—one of the oldest discipline of science.

The word *surgery* comes from the Greek word *kheirourgia* meaning 'working or done by hand' and the closely related word *anatomy* comes from the Greek word, which means to 'cut open'. Even though trephination existing over 8,000 years in early Neolithic and pre-Classical ages, it was Herophilus of Chalcedon and Erasistrus of Cos in the third century BC that carried out the first dissection and study of corpses. But later, it was a child who was introduced to the healing arts by his father that turned out to be the father of modern medicine, the Hippocrates of Cos. He travelled through Greece and the Asia Minor as a travelling doctor and published *Corpus Hippocratium*, which is even now used to understand the healing methods of antiquity. He was responsible for the whole new way of thinking in medicine and his approach made his work seem almost modern. He tried to recognise the causes of illness by objective scientific examination rather than irrational, magical, and religious healing methods, which were practised at his times. He also established the theory of four cardinal humours which established that the body falls ill when there is an imbalance in the bodily fluids. No longer the disease was treated as a curse from god, but the result of natural causes and could be treated with natural remedies. The importance of his work is seen in the Hippocrates Oath, which is taken by the doctors and his works has been vital to the understanding of the ancient art of healing.

Later, the physiology developed under the principles of Hippocrates, but the science of anatomy lay dormant till the fourteenth century due to the religious ban on dissecting a corpus. The surgeon Andreas Vesalius, the founding father of modern surgery and a professor in Padua, was one of the first to apply scientific thoughts to the anatomy. Rather than believing in ancient writings, he believed on what he saw with his eyes. He published his works on hearts, veins, arteries, and skeletons after learning from the dissection of corpses. His lifetime work, seven books on the structure of human body, is the theoretical foundation of modern medicine. He was given the nickname Vesanus (the mad man), since he questioned most of the existing theories of that time. All the most important discoveries in the medicine owe the debt to Vesalius who changed the face of medicine, which saw man as the centre since antiquity. In 1543, he wrote the groundbreaking *De Humani Corporis Fabrica Libri Septem*, which became the most comprehensive anatomy text at the time and the basis for 200 years of anatomical study. Even though Vesalius opened the arena of dissection, till the seventh century scientists believed the church and the dissection of autopsies were considered as evil omen.

However, in the seventeenth century, the church recognised the importance of studying the dead for the benefit of the living. Even the Greek doctor Galen defined pathology as the study of suffering. The study of diseases, as we see today, goes back to Giovani Battista Morgagni from Padua. His five-volume book on the seats and causes of sickness that came out in 1760 was the result of 700 autopsies he had conducted as part of his pathological research. For the first time in the history of mankind, Morgagni demonstrated the relationship between the symptoms of disease, causes of disease, and the findings of the postmortem. He defined the correlation between the illness and the specific changes found in human organs. The school of thought was welcomed by the doctors, but they started to get reproached as grave robbers, as they worked on the cadavers. Moreover, when they were done with the bodies, they themselves were responsible for disposing the corpses off.

Then most of the professors started to restrict themselves from the corpses and focused more on textbooks. Soon in eighteenth century, the hospital and universities realised the importance of having the prosectors, especially for dissection, and started to hire them. While the professors gave the anatomy lectures, these specialists pinpointed to the specific topics and anatomical change in the body. This was the beginning of the modern course on surgery. While shifts in anatomical knowledge empowered surgeons, many procedures remained out of reach.

Physicians could not attempt complex internal surgery or prolonged operations. There were two simple inventions that enabled the surgeries as we see today. One was washing hands (on a lighter note) using carbolic acid by Joseph Lister, and the second was the development of ether gas for anaesthesia. The sky was the limit, and the surgery could be done on any place and the surgeons became gods, but at a cost of the patients who lost their well-being, as it took ages to recover from the wounds from surgery. By the twentieth century, asepsis, or the prevention of bacteria from entering a wound or sterile environment, gained prominence. Through methods such as boiling, using autoclaves, and chemical antiseptics, sterile operating environments were achieved. Physicians began wearing white coats, and clean linens dressed beds and operating tables.

The knowledge of blood group-typing and transfusion techniques, understanding of blood clotting and the use of anticoagulants were the next leg of the medical evolution.

But where did we learn about the blood—the most critical element of the physiology of human? The theory of circulation of the blood in the human body was first postulated by Greek physician, Galen, who described the word pathology in his works. According to him, nutrients were conveyed along the intestines to liver, and it was the liver that converted the nutrients to new blood as the old blood seeped away. Galen was also convinced that there are two types of blood vessels: one that carries good blood, and other that carry impure blood to the heart. He claimed that there were tiny pores in the thick muscular partition. He served for three years as doctor to Roman gladiators, and as the emperor's surgeon, gaining hands-on surgical experience.

Romans continued with trephining, amputations, and eye surgery. After Galen's death, physicians and anatomists still believed that there existed the pores for around 1,800 years. Even though there were distributed thoughts on the distribution of blood, it was William Harvey, the physician of the English court, who developed the first convincing theory on the circulation of blood, disproving the belief that liver was the centre of circulation of blood. In 1628, he refuted all the existing beliefs by publishing the *De Mortu Cordis* (The Movement of Heart), which was completely based on the observations he made through experiments and anatomical dissections. In his book, he described two circulatory systems: one form the heart through the body and back (the systemic circulation), and the other from the heart to lungs and back (the pulmonary circulation). He also could prove the pumping mechanism of the heart and the role of valves that enabled the circulation in a single direction.

The puzzle of how the blood from the arteries end up in veins was finally solved by Marcello Malpighi who first discovered the existence of capillaries, and expressed the opinion of the existence of a large, widely branching network of blood vessels. The discovery of the human blood circulatory system opened up new possibilities in the field of medicine such as intravenous injections and blood transfusion. Even though there were trials in blood transfusion by Jean Baptiste Dennis by giving the sheep's blood to a patient, resulting in fatal complications, the full-fledged blood transfusion started with the discovery of blood groups in 1901 by Karl Landsteiner who found out that the blood of two people under contact agglutinates—an effect due to contact of blood with blood serum. He identified the three blood groups *A*, *B*, and *O*, and with his claim that blood transfusion between persons with the same blood group will not lead to the destruction of blood cells, in 1907, the first successful blood transfusion was performed by Reuben Ottenberg at Mount Sinai Hospital in New York.

But even then the composition of the blood was unknown to the medical world. In 1668, Antonie van Leewenhoek, who worked with microscopes that magnified objects, was the first one to see the red blood corpuscles after getting inspired by the work of William Harvey and Malpighi. He also observed the red blood corpuscles flowing through the capillaries of rabbit's ear and frog's leg. His insights into the structure of blood are still the basic knowledge of medicine. He wrote all his findings in Dutch and kept his outstanding lenses resolutely, even taking his knowledge of the lenses to the grave.

Though he identified the structure, one concept still lied unexplained. Most of the research on human body had its origins on the experiments on animals. In 1726, an English clergyman, Stephen Hales, performed an animal experiment by introducing a thin brass tube into the carotid artery of mare. This tube was connected to a ten-feet long vertical glass tube, and the blood pressure of the mare pushed the blood unto a height of six feet. The blood in the tube moved in sync with the heartbeat. He also noted that the highest pressure is noted when the heart is contracting. The lowest pressure represented the level of resistance presented by the blood vessels in the body. Even though this was an invasive method of measurement, based on this principle, in 1881, a Viennese university lecturer Ritten von Basch invented sphygmomanometer. It has a balloon that constricted the flow of the blood in the arm and measured the pressure when the pulse disappeared. At the turn of the century, blood was the indicator of strength of heart rather than the pressure generated. Hence, high blood pressure was considered mistakenly as the sign of good health.

The frills, as we see on the instrument such as the mercury manometer, was added by an Italian paediatrician, Scipione Rocci. It was only in 1905 that a Russian surgeon, Nocolai Sergejewitsch, identified that by reducing the pressure on the balloon, and thus reinitiating flow of the blood we can measure the blood pressure when the heart relaxes. The experiment of Stephen Hales on the live mare contributed significantly on the progress of non-invasive health monitoring which was a breakthrough in the history of medicine.

The understanding of the development of human being from the embryo to the fully-grown kid in the uterus was another landmark in the medical history. The Greek doctor, Hippocrates, believed that the male created the soul of the man and the role of mother was only to give the physical form for the seed provided by the man. This pre-formation theory held strong till the sixteenth century AD since the church prevented any biological research on the evolution of human life. When the religious restrictions were loosened during the reformation, doctor Hieronymus Fabricius studied the embryonic development in more detail using the chicken eggs. With the recently developed microscope, he revealed previously unseen developments. In 1600, he published his work under the name *De Format Foetu* in which for the first time, the role of placenta and the umbilical cord was described. It was this work that inspired William Harvey who observed the development of the internal organs of the foetus. The work of Fabricius and Harvey on the embryo paved the way to the development of the modern theory of evolution.

But have you ever thought when did the habit of seeing a doctor came into our culture? Sickness and injury have always troubled humanity from the beginning of times. When people fell sick, they knew to use the emetics and laxatives, but later they started using medical equipment to measure the vitals of human body.

Technology of medical instruments developed along with modern science. The stream that helped played an important role in the development of modern medical instruments was the optics. In the antiquity, there were two conflicting theories about the generation, nature, propagation, and reception of light. The emission theory that assumed that human eyes send out sight rays, which collided with the object whose image they brought back to the eyes. On the contrary, an unknown phenomenon was produced by the object that then simulated the eye to give the sensation of sight. It was in AD 1,000 that the scholar name Abu Ali Alhazen became interested in the theory of sight, and described the anatomy of the eye. He was the person who proved that the sight was the perception felt by the eye when the reflected light is recede by the eye.

He defined the reflection and refraction of light. His work paved the way to the invention of spectacles, and later, the modern theory of light developed by Johan Kepler. Alhazen work was reined by Ezam Vitello around 1250s. At about the same time, clear minerals were used as vision aids. Clear segments were cut from the polished quart or beryl, flat on one side, and curved outside on the other side. The flat side was used to move on the letters so that the letters would be enlarged. Later, this principle was set on a metal or wooden frame and started to be used as the magnifying glass. In the late thirteenth century, Alessandro di Spina from Pisa developed the idea of joining two glasses by riveting the handles of frames and clamping the support on the nose. This opened up a new aid to enable vision for many people who tend to decrease the eyesight after forty-five.

The industry of the spectacle makers started to thrive, and an idea came to the mind of kid who was fascinated by his father's work on spectacles. It was Zacharias Janssen, whose father was a renowned spectacle maker, Hans. Janssen's pioneering work was inspired by the thought that if the glass could enable the people to get a better vision, why not use the same glass to magnify the objects we find difficult to see with our naked eye? The pioneering result of their work came in 1590 in which they described an apparatus, consisting of two lenses and three tubings, the first compound microscope. This revolutionary invention changed the world of medicine and science. The details of nature that he couldn't see through his naked eye opened up in front of him. Suddenly, the whole new unknown world, which was once beyond his vision limits, was conquered. Later in early 1700s, an amateur scientist, Leewenhoek, developed new techniques to improve the microscopy by rectifying the chromatic aberration, and increasing the magnifying power of the instrument unto 300 times. This magnificent invention opened out the avenues for scientific research, and now the scientist are able to open up the structure of the atoms with the electron microscope with a resolute of less than 0.2 nanometers.

Applying the same principles, followed by the spectacle makers, the mathematician, Hans Lippershey, made a Dutch telescope in 1608 and applied for a patent. When Galileo heard about this invention, he mounted a convex and concave lense in pipes of different circumference, and used as a telescope to see the heavens, and thus made some remarkable discoveries. He became the first person to observe the moon and make comments about its surface. By refining this telescope, he could even reach the Jupiter and its four moons, discovery of which overthrew the hypothesis of Ptolemy on the geocentricity. Galileo published his discoveries in the book *Message from the Stars*. He underlined his discoveries in his later book, *The Dialogo*, which ignited the fury of the church. Under the threat of torture, he was forced to repudiate the teachings of Copernicus, and later was put on house arrest.

All these aggressions by the church couldn't halt the progress of inventions, and with these inventions, it became possible to prove that the heliocentric model about the solar system was correct. Till the time of Aristotle, it was considered as the bow of the God, which he created as a treaty of peace with the mankind. But Aristotle believed that some sort of optical effect caused the reflection and refraction of the sun's rays. But it was the Polish natural scientist, Witelo, in the end of thirteenth century, who came close the actual explanation of the theory of rainbow. He explained that when the sun shines through a raindrop, the light is refracted on the surface of the drop. He also gave the order in which the colours appeared. The complete explanation of the phenomenon was given by the Dominican monk, Dietrich von Freiburg, even on the shape of the rainbow. In the seventeenth century, the French mathematician, Rene Descartes, substantiated the theory of Freiburg by mathematical support of the theory of dispersion and refraction.

Another natural phenomenon that found explanation over the same time was the mystery of the lightning. It was once believed that the lightning was the expression of God's anger, since it caused disastrous damage. People believed that the lightning was extremely random, and they couldn't protect themselves from it. The invention of the lightning conductor changed the view completely. It was an accidental discovery by Benjamin Franklin in 1752. A summer thunderstorm gave him an idea of the same. He got an electric shock when he was flying a kite in the thunderstorm. Understanding that the lightning is an electric phenomenon, he decided to attract lightning through an iron rod fitted with a steel tip, projecting over six feet above the roof, and the other end of the rod buried five feet deep in the ground. The system was accepted widely in America. The system was simple to install and gave effective protection against the damages from lightning. Even the church, which opposed the installation of the system against the wonders of God, accepted the system to protect its tall steeples.

Franklin had proposed a pointed edge at the top end, and there is an interesting story behind the same getting transformed to a round end. The British king, George III, deplored Franklin so much as a fighter for American independence that his invention should not be uncritically adopted. So he insisted that the lightning conductors at his palaces should have rounded ends rather than Franklin's pointed ones.

Ironically, it was found in the later twentieth century that the rounded end construction was more effective. The optics and electricity revolutionised the path of medical history by paving way for the development of sophisticated, meticulously designed devices. The development of this combination opened a new path for development. Electrically powered surgical instruments became invaluable for cauterization and for separating hard tissues such as bone with minimal damage. The advent of surgical stapling instruments that evolved in the Soviet Union joined blood vessels or other tissues in less than half the time required by hand stitching. The new inventions such as medical glues, surgical tapes, and even zippers now enable surgeons to close some wounds effectively without stitches. With the development of optics with the combination of electricity accelerated, the development of X-rays and fluoroscopy. The computerized axial tomography (CAT) scans and magnetic resonance imaging (MRI), surgery gained valuable diagnostic instruments. These technologies led the way to operations that are conducted inside specially adapted MRI devices, allowing the surgeon to have live images for guidance during operations.

We have the holograms that can be created using data from MRI and diagnostic instruments, and are beginning to be used in the operating room to give surgeons a three-dimensional image of the area to be operated upon. Cryogenic, or supercooled probe beams, have been used to precisely remove tissues and abnormal growths. Then we started using ultrasound techniques to break up kidney stones, and employed scanning mechanisms in brain and ear operations for improved precision and control. With the advent of medical lasers, which produced amplified monochromatic light waves as a very narrowly focused beam, the technology has enabled spot-welding of tissues.

The heart–lung machine made open-heart surgery possible by taking over the blood-pumping and breathing functions of these organs during operations. Hypothermia or cold surgery—by which the body is cooled to lower the rate of metabolism, thus reducing the need for oxygen—has made long operations, especially those involving transplantation, possible. Other recent transplantation advances include procedures involving the liver, lungs, pancreas, bone marrow, and the kidney. After the first human heart transplant was performed in 1967 by South African surgeon Christiaan Barnard, we have even reached a stage in which as I am writing the book, we have the first brain transplant to be done on Valery Spiridonov performed by Italian neurosurgeon Sergio Canavero. During the procedure, estimated to last about thirty-six hours, Spiridonov's head will be cooled to around twelve degrees Celsius, cut from his body and, as quickly as possible, connected to a donated body of a brain-dead person. It is expected to be done by a team of 100 surgeons and other medical staff, including some who have experience in head transplants on animals.

Mechanics of human body, the orthopaedics, was also introduced, with the use of cementing substances to unite bones destroyed by tumour and the replacement of joints with metal or plastic devices. Plastic surgery and reconstructive surgery have made enormous strides, and microsurgery is making severed or injured limbs usable. A trend towards less invasive surgery and shorter hospital stays began in the 1980s. By 1995, more than 56 per cent of all surgical procedures in the United States were done on an outpatient basis without an overnight stay in a hospital. Endoscopic surgery, using small incisions and tiny instruments attached to fibre optic viewing devices, has been used in place of more traditional procedures for gallbladder surgery, and it has been used on the fetus in the womb to correct life-threatening birth defects before birth. Angioplasty is frequently used to circumvent or postpone the need for coronary artery bypass. Today, in India alone, we perform 265 million surgeries every year, which requires around four crore units of blood every year, which would increase at an average of over 12 per cent every year.

Out of all these recent developments, the best story that I had heard was that of an 'aspirational' techno geek of Hong Kong who made a Scarlett Johansson (ScarJo bot) clone. I mean a robotic clone. Though this bot can be the future of objectifying women, I would be happy if I were greeted by one of them when I step into a hotel (which I cannot say in front of my wife though). But what have we achieved so far from the bionic technology? According to the creator of the ScarJo bot, it took eighteen months and just over US$50,000 to complete this amazing project in his patio with a 3D printer and the self-learned software. Moreover, our Siri is a woman and our Cortana is also a woman! On a lighter note, if a bot would exist to perform labour or any personal assistance, I bet it would be a woman, and I felt it is so obvious with our physiological and evolutionary requirements.

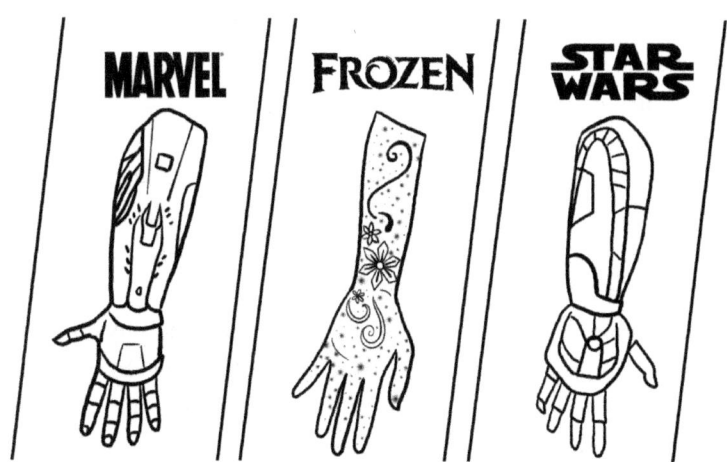

This is the new era of bionics. Bionics is defined as anatomical structures or physiological processes that are replaced or enhanced by electronic or mechanical components, which would assist in acquiring extraordinary powers or capabilities of being a superhuman. Bridging the gap between man and machine once a science fantasy is now a global industry. In the age when Europe is lacking people to work in their fabulous factories, and China thrashing up its one-child policy, considering the exploding old-age population, do we need to think an alternate through the bionic humans powered by artificial intelligence? Tomorrow, I might have a bionic human in the family—a cybernetic organism (a cyborg) that knows more about me than I know about myself. These organisms would be a complex hybrid system (may be living or non-living, I am not sure how we will draw the line between living and non-living) combining biological and engineering parts.

With the current technology that could control the limbs with the thoughts alone, just as the way in which our limb performs, the extended application of such a technology is limitless. As I had always dreamt during my examinations about getting the access to my classroom notes just through a pen drive plugged into the brain, I believe this possibility is not as far as we think. In future, except the logical decisions that we could take considering the information available, the rest of the data can be loaded and unloaded to the brain as we need.

From the time when amputated humans were assisted with the twigs from the tree to the intelligent eyes that helped the blind to understand the colours of the world, we have made an immense progress in bionics technology. In the new era of the machines when humans are required to satisfy the social and physiological needs of humans, we could see a transformed era of bionics, which can reduce the impact of ageing and make the older more mobile. Will this increase the retirement age? Need to wait and see.

As the elderly population grows, so is the global bionic industry. Extending the life of ageing limbs and the functioning of the damaged ones, in the next five years, this industry is expected to grow over twenty billion unless there is a disruptive breakthrough. If such a breakthrough happens, it will be much bigger. By 2050, it is expected that the elderly population of the world would be around 16 per cent (around 1.5 billion). In developing countries, such as China, the older population (those over age 65) is likely to swell from 110 million today to 330 million by 2050, and that of India from 60 million to 227 million. The key problems for the elderly include the lack of mobility and the companionship. If the new bionics age is able to address these growing needs of the population, it would be the next game-changing field for the years to come.

The bionics will also level the playing field between the physically challenged people and the common human. More than one billion people have some form of disability. This corresponds to about 15 per cent of the world's population. The key disabilities for them are related to the vision and the mobility that are being addressed as we speak. If such new technologies become scalable, and mass production of these inventions is achieved, they would turn out to be a boon for the amputated and disabled.

Another possibility is to look at the need for a mechanised organ that could be developed through the technology. The current transplantation covers only 10 per cent of the global need. Either the world has to move to an organised organ market to curb the black market of the organ smugglers, or it should find a biological or mechanical source through technology to build a stockpile of bionic organs that would address the growing global organ demand.

So we should be ready to accept a new family member who could help us in our old age, and possibly a limb or an organ that would be a machine to be part of our aura. The blend of man and machine of the future would be a necessary transition for the generations to come, and thus see ourselves as civilised and rational cyborgs. Even the organ printing, which was just a scientific fiction, is a matter a reality today. The idea that a broken piece of ourselves might be replaced with a healthy piece, or a piece from somebody else, stretches back centuries. Cosmas and Damian, Roman surgeons, have attached the leg of a deceased Ethiopian Moor onto a white Roman in the third century AD. In 1905, the ophthalmologist, Eduard Zirm, successfully cut a cornea from an injured 11-year-old boy, and emigrated it into the body of a 45-year-old Czech farm labourer whose eyes had been damaged while he was slaking lime. A decade later, Sir Harold Gillies, sometimes called a founding father of plastic surgery, performed skin grafts on British soldiers during World War I. But the first successful transplant of a major organ—an organ vital to human function—didn't happen until 1954 when Ronald Herrick, a 23-year-old from Massachusetts, donated one of his healthy kidneys to his twin brother, Richard, who was suffering from chronic nephritis.

Going much further, we have successfully bioprinted skin, bone, muscle, cartilage, and kidney structures; and in immediate future, we would be having bioengineered organs. Furthermore, we do not even know how will the maverick Italian scientist, Dr Sergio Canavero, conducting the head transplant, will go. If it is successful, it would be first step to human eternity.

On the other hand of eternity is what we would see in eternity through the gene modification. We will soon have the option to make genetically modified kids based on our interest—the designer babies. These babies will be perfect to the best extent possible. The new type of genetic engineering known as CRISPR (acronym for Clustered Regularly Interspaced Short Palindromic Repeat refers to short sections of repeating DNA in bacteria or other microorganisms) system offers a huge potential in editing genomes with the possibility of removing faulty genes and replacing them with functional ones, rewriting muscular dystrophy genes, or protecting us from tropical diseases like normal cough and cold. We will dig a little deep to understand how bacterial immune system works. When a virus invades a bacterium, it replicates its DNA until it completely takes over the cell. But the bacterium has to stop the replication in order to survive. To do that, it must destroy the viral genome, and this is where the CRISPR system comes in. Inside bacterium, there are small DNA parts called spacers, which contain the information on the viruses that have previously attacked. This alerts the bacterium on the attack. But if the virus is new, the viral DNA must first be placed into the CRISPR sequence as a new spacer.

Once that's done, the viral DNA is copied into an RNA molecule, activating CRISPR-associated proteins. These are the immune system elements that enter the RNA molecule, attack viral DNA and cut it in half to prevent replication. This system is applied to humans and other animals to adjust genes, remove mutations, or even add completely new ones. It's a powerful system that has huge implications for the future of genetic engineering, which can lead to designer babies or the development of perfect humans. If the in vitro fertilisation technique can bring five million smiles in the world within four decades, genetic modification technique will modify the way in which we see our generations.

Another technology that would see the development of biological revolution is the organ transplantation. Humans have around 10 different organs in our body that can be transplanted. These include kidneys, heart, liver, pancreas, intestines, lungs, bones, bone marrow, skin, and corneas. As per the Donate Life Foundation, 80% of the global organ demand constitute the kidneys with an average wait time of over 3 years. In 2016, for the first time, the organ transplants performed in the United States alone crossed 30,000. But, as we speak approximately four times of that number still awaits lifesaving organ transplants. Furthermore, around 22 people die every day waiting for an organ. From an Indian perspective, 5 lakh people across the India die each year due to non-availability of organs. One out five need a liver, but only one in hundred receive it. Two out of five need a kidney, but only one in twenty receive it. Even though 8-10 brain dead potential donors are available in Intensive Care Units of any major city hospitals around the globe, the taboo of the donation still constrain the effectiveness of donation. Right after identifying the pluripotency (ability to develop to different organs) of stem cells after cloning Dolly, bio-engineering has gone to a different level of creativity. In March 2017, Organovo world's first publicly traded 3D bio-printing company, announced the medical success of the bio-printed liver and kidney with promising results. Like the complex, multi-cellular tissues found within a person, these human tissues are created through cell division; they mature and integrate into the tissue, forming connections with surrounding cells and contributing functionality throughout their lifespan. As individual cells within the tissue age, they eventually undergo cellular senescence and death—much as they would in a living tissue inside the body. This is the ultimate approach to the shortage of donor organs – manufacture and transplantation of bio-artificial organs. The latest trend is the chimera – a mixture of cells from more than one species growing together as a single animal – resulting in human organs being produced in other animals. A chimera, named after the cross-species beast of Greek mythology, is essentially a single organism that's made up of cells from two or more "individuals"—that is, it contains two sets of DNA, with the code to make two separate organisms. One way that chimeras can happen naturally in humans is that a fetus can absorb its twin. This can occur with fraternal twins, if one embryo dies very early in pregnancy, and some of its cells are "absorbed" by the other twin. The remaining fetus will have two sets of cells, its own original set, plus the one from its twin. Another way this can happen is when a person undergoes a bone marrow transplant, especially during the treatment of leukemia. After the treatment the person will have their own bone marrow destroyed and replaced with bone marrow from another person. Bone marrow contains stem cells that develop into red blood cells. This means that a person with a bone marrow transplant will have blood cells, for the rest of their life, that are genetically identical to those of the donor, and are not genetically the same as the other cells in their own body.

This technique has been tweaked to fit to a specific requirement – to harvest human organs. The paper, published in the journal Cell in Jan 2017, outlines how human stem cells were injected into early-stage pig embryos, resulting in more than 2,000 hybrids that were transferred to surrogate sows. More than 150 of the embryos developed into chimeras that were mostly pig, but with a tiny human contribution of around one in 10,000 cells. The team believe that in future the approach could pave the way for incubating human organs, genetically matched to a patient, for use in transplants or for testing new medicines more safely and effectively. Even though the study has reignited ethical concerns, by perfecting the art of growing such chimeric replacement livers, kidneys and pancreases inside the animal hosts, the organ shortage may end. It may so happen that we may be ordering a homo-porcine kidney on Amazon soon by end of this decade. Gone are the painful days for the organ donor.

This could even be applicable in the case of developing designer babies too from for the infertile women. The study by Northwestern University Feinberg School of Medicine and McCormick School of Engineering found that by removing a female mouse' ovary and replacing it with a bioprosthetic ovary, the mouse was able to not only ovulate but also give birth to healthy pups. The moms were even able to nurse their young.

These bioprosthetic ovaries are constructed of 3-D printed scaffolds that house immature eggs, and have been successful in boosting hormone production and restoring fertility in mice, which was the ultimate goal of the research. This will help restore fertility in women who have undergone adult cancer treatments or those who survived childhood cancer and now have increased risks of infertility and hormone-based developmental issues. Won't that be so sweet for our new generation mothers?

After the defeat of Lee Sedol by the AlphaGo, and the winning of the poker by the intelligent robot, I have started losing sleep on the thoughts of the evolution of machine intelligence. I don't think anybody should, but let us see whether the news is worth pondering.

The game Go is from China. It is a simple game with black and white stones on the board in which the players try to capture the opponent's stones, or surround empty space to make points of territory. Though the rules are simple, it is jaw-droppingly complex. As per the mathematicians, there are more positions in Go that there are atoms in the universe. Did you get the number? If not, it is googol times complex than chess. Still you did not get it, it is defined as one followed by 100 zeros.

This game has been considered the most challenging classical games for artificial intelligence, owing to the enormous space and difficulty of deriving the positions and the moves. This was an epic game in which a computer program defeated a professional human player, which was previously considered at least a decade away.

I think with the advent of this victory, we are concurring to the dangers that Nick Bostrom, the global authority on superintelligence, had his concerns on. According to him, the development of superintelligence may pose an existential risk to humanity over the coming century. We would not be a match for the evolving machines. The cognitive performance of these machines would considerably exceed the capacity of all the mankind put together. Is there a way out from this catastrophe?

The superintelligence is a baby that is being conceived by the defeat of Lee Sedol, but it should not be the defeat of the humanity. As the guardians of the concept, the thought leaders have the moral responsibility to ensure an ethical application of science. I believe we, as a mankind, should drive science to reduce the existential risk of humanity, and use the superintelligence to protect the humanity from the existential risks posed by the nature or any other similar technologies.

A baby is never born criminal; it is the environment and the people who mold it are responsible for the behaviour. Will our generations venerate us for developing the ethical sense on machines, or would they curse us for making a Frankenstein monster?

Year 2030, I was just roaming in my garden. My youngest daughter, Annie, was playing in the ground in the see-saw. Hair soft, silky hair was flying in the gentle wind. She had a runny nose, not the brightest student in the class, not the most elegant in the crowd, of course, my kid my generation. On the other side, her best friend, Emmy, was a designer baby. She never had the runny nose unlike my kid, she was the brightest, and was one of the most elegant among the crowd, and she had the coolest playmate, Julie, which was a superintelligent machine. But is she the generation of her parents and will my lineage be among the fittest to survive?

8

BESIDES BLACK ART, THERE IS ONLY AUTOMATION AND MECHANISATION

Today, I woke up early in the morning for my jogging. I heard the milk cooker in my nearby home whistling so well that it was almost like my second alarm. Was this just the power of steam that marked the growth of human brain? Yes. Whistling kettle, in fact, was one of the crude inventions that had harnessed the power of steam.

In eighteenth century, when the English blacksmith, Thomas Newcomen, built the first efficient steam engine, it marked the beginning of the new era of industrialisation, changing the life of people fundamentally and permanently and the exponential growth of human brain power, and thus his intelligence quotient. The Newcomen engine worked by using the air pressure. The pump linkage was connected to a piston inside the cylinder in such a way that the weight of the linkage forced the piston upwards. At the same time, steam was admitted to the cylinder from a separate boiler. With the piston in the upper position, the steam was cut off and condensed by cold water, causing a vacuum inside the cylinder; thereby, the atmospheric air pushed the piston down again. This caused the pump linkage to rise. This mechanism was a blessing for miners for removing water from mines. John Smeaton made a refinement on the engine, reducing the coal consumption by 50 per cent, and the engine was adopted across the mines throughout Britain.

It was mere coincidences that led the further development of the engine. An engine mechanic, James Watt, while he was repairing one of the Newcomen engines, noticed that the alternate cycles of heating and cooling, if avoided, could reduce the consumption even further. On 5 January 1769, he applied for his patent to keep a separate condenser in the engine so that the engine cylinder and the condenser always remained at the same hot and cool temperatures. This was a breakthrough invention, and he could bring down the consumption of coal to one-quarter of the earlier Newcomen engine. Soon, he started to rent out his machine at one-third of the cost of the coal saved. His business partner, Mathew Boulton, expressed their view in a very candid statement, 'I sell what the whole world wants to have—power.' It was a historical statement and it was true. That was the beginning of the new industrial era.

When the civilisation was getting emerged in the larger scale, in the household settlements, there was another fundamental need emerged, which is even thriving till today. The wearing of clothing is exclusively a human characteristic and is a feature of most human societies. It is not known when humans began wearing clothes, but anthropologists believe that animal skins and vegetation were adapted into coverings as protection from cold, heat, and rain, especially as humans migrated to new climates from the cradle of evolution. Evidence suggests that humans may have begun wearing clothing as far back as 10,000 to 50,000 years ago.

The use of needles enabled the usage of clothing in the style in which it is worn today. The earliest evidence of weaving comes from impressions of textiles and basketry, and nets on little pieces of hard clay, dating from 27,000 years ago. According to the climate, the sense of fashion, as we see today, changed. The Europe emerged as people adorned with basket hats or caps, belts worn at the waist, and a strap of cloth that wrapped around the body right above the breast. In the tropics, there was cotton. The inhabitants of the Indus Valley civilisation used cotton for clothing as early as the 5th–4th millennium BC. Evidence exists for production of linen cloth in Ancient Egypt in the Neolithic period, 5,500 BC. The earliest evidence of silk production in China was between 5,000 and 3,000 BC. The invention of woven clothes opened up a whole new window of global trade, social status, and fashion. The use of clothes transformed from the simple requirement of protection from the sun, cold, rain, and heat to an integral part of human lifestyle.

The abundance such clothes was one reason for the modern trade. Even though the trade had originated with human communication in prehistoric times in which people bartered goods and services from each other before the innovation of modern-day currency, the trade routes were the result of such exquisite materials. When the trade started with various civilisations, it was with the exchange of obsidian (naturally occurring volcanic glass), flint (form of mineral quartz), Lapis lazuli (a deep blue semi-precious stone prized for its colour) during the Stone Age in South West Asia.

Long-range trade routes first appeared in the third millennium BCE when Sumerians in Mesopotamia traded with the Harappan civilisation of the Indus Valley. From the beginning of Greek civilisation until the fall of the Roman empire in the fifth century, trade brought valuable spice and silk to Europe from the Far East including India and China. This was the beginning of the Silk Route. Geographically, the Silk Road or Silk Route is an interconnected series of ancient trade routes between China with Asia Minor and the Mediterranean extending over 8,000 km on land and sea. Trade on the Silk Road was a significant factor in the development of the great civilisations of China, Egypt, Mesopotamia, Persia, the Indian subcontinent, and Rome, and helped to lay the foundations for the modern world.

The discovery of natural dyes and the use of silk by the Chinese added an extraordinary charm to the adornment. In 2,500 BC, the

Chinese emperor, Huang Ti, developed the silk-weaving and the embroidery, as we see now in the Chinese silk. In addition to the same, spinning was one of the basic skills that was developed by the ancient civilisation. In order to achieve a long, continuous thread from the short thread, men had to achieve an uninterrupted rotary movement in the same direction. Even though the spinning wharve dates from 5,000 BC, it was around 1,000 BC that the Chinese and the Indians developed the crude form of spinning wheel. When the Chinese used to make the silk threads, Indians used to make cotton. Like weaving, the spinning also was the work of women, and she had the responsibility of making clothes for the family. The development of the spinning wheel reduced their effort considerably. Once the industrial revolution hit mankind, the spinning jenny was invented, which revolutionised the entire cloth-making industry.

The textile industry, which was always the driving force in economic development, was the first to use the Watts engine by mechanising the spinning machines and, soon, the loom. Though this marked the emergence of the industrialisation, it also marked the beginning of grim factory towns in which child labour, low wages, and long hours were the predominant characteristics.

It was with the development of the mechanical spinning machine, the flying shuttle by John Kay, in which the shuttle was enabled to move faster through the gap between the warp threads, thus accelerating the process of weaving, the world stepped into the era of automation. This resulted in the production of more fabric, and demand of yarn skyrocketed. To satisfy the demand of the same, the spinning mills started looking ways to speed up their production. In 1767, James Hargreaves invented the spinning jenny, which he named after his daughter. Instead of the common standard of one spindle of yarn, this mechanical spinning mill could simultaneously spin eight threads. Two years later, Richard Arkwright constructed a spinning mill with an automatic feed; and by 1785, the machine was steam-powered.

This invention took the textile industry to the next level. Orders started pouring with the flourishing of the English cotton, and with the international trade, he became the greatest textile manufacturer of his time. But the industry was yet to graduate to the power loom. In 1806, an English country parson, Edmund Cartwright, perfected the technology of power loom powered by steam. This enabled the cotton cloth production in unbelievable quantities. With slight adjustments, the loom could even produce wool, flax, and silk. By the middle of nineteenth century, there were more than 75,000 power looms just in Britain, Scotland, and Wales.

The invention of power looms was the death knell for the traditional cottage industry of weaving. Production moved from traditional place from homes into factories, and factory cities worsening the working conditions of weavers. The workers united and put up a struggle, and the best known example for the same was the revolt of the weavers of Silesia in1844. Crowds of weavers attacked homes and warehouses, destroyed machinery, and demanded money from local merchants. In response, the Prussian Army was called to restore order in the region. In confrontations between the weavers and troops, shots were fired into the crowd and people died. In many ways, the Silesian weavers' revolt was a traditional response to poverty and hunger. The start of the industrialisation marked the beginning of the unequal distribution of income. This event has gained the impetus for labour movement in England and Germany. In particular, Karl Marx regarded the uprising as evidence of the birth of workers' movement.

Another invention that made life simple for the women was the invention of windmills. Cereals have been a basic food for the mankind since 10,000 years. Initially, the cereals were placed on a larger stone, and the women crushed the same with a smaller stone. Later, mills were rotated by handle and had a built-in funnel in the upper millstone for filling even while the stone was getting turned.

By the first century AD, man started using animals to rotate the shafts of mills, and started using the power to water to turn the wheels. Persians were the first to notice the power of the wind, since they were seafaring people. They made the first windmill in AD 915 in the Persian province of Sistan. The sails outside drove the vertical shaft, which was, in turn, connected to the mill for the grinding. By the end of twelfth century, it had flourished to the European society; and by the fourteenth century, large stationary windmills started appearing across the world. By the arrival of steam engine, the prominence of windmill was lost completely.

While the industrialisation was in progress in one part of the world, there was another part of the world where some different machines were getting made. Perhaps the first example of a human-made device designed to manage power is the hand axe made by chipping flint to form a wedge—there were few artistic depictions on how the power to be managed. If we look at the evolution of automation, the drivers behind it either was to assist or entertain human or to replace human. There are many examples in the Hellenic World mainly intended to be tools, toys, religious idols, or prototypes for demonstrating basic scientific principles

But the power management, or the automation in principle, was evolved by the ancient Greek engineer, Hero of Alexandria, who produced two texts, Pneumatica and Automata—the wonder machines. Among his most famous inventions was the wind wheel, constituting the earliest instance of wind harnessing on land. Over and above, Hero published a well-recognised description of a steam-powered rocket-like reaction engine device called an aeolipile (sometimes called a 'Hero engine'). The fact to note is that it was created almost two millennia before the industrial revolution.

Another invention was that engine used air from a closed chamber heated by an altar fire to displace water from a sealed vessel. The water was collected, and its weight, pulling on a rope, opened temple doors. Some historians have conflated the two inventions to assert that the aeolipile was capable of useful work. There were complex mechanical devices known to have existed in Hellenistic Greece as part of entertainment too, though the only oldest surviving example is the Antikythera mechanism, the earliest known analog computer to predict astronomical positions and eclipses for calendrical and astrological purposes.

Even before there were legendary depictions of the Jewish legend, Solomon designed a throne with mechanical animals, which hailed him as king when he ascended it. The Indian king, Ajatashatru of Magadha, who gathered the Buddha's relics and hid them in an underground stupa, were protected by mechanical robots (*bhuta vahana yantra*) from the kingdom of Roma Visaya until they were disarmed by King Ashoka. In Ancient China, a mechanical engineer known as Yan Shi presented the king with a life-size human-shaped figure. Greek mathematician, Archytas of Tarentum, built a mechanical bird dubbed 'the Pigeon'. The Pigeon was propelled by steam and could fly a distance of 200 metres. In the Medieval period, similar automata continued with singing birds, roaring and moving lions; and in the mid-eighth century, the first wind-powered automata were built—statues that turned with the wind in the city of Baghdad.

The humanoid connection of the automatons was made by Arab polymath, Al-Jazari. In this book, *The Book of Knowledge of Ingenious Mechanical Devices*, he described 100 mechanical devices, along with instructions on how to construct them. He was the epitome of practical engineering that could be done with the available techniques of that era. His automatons included the mechanisms that are even used today such as Camshaft, Crankshaft, crank-slider mechanism, mechanical controls, and gear. He also used double-action suction pump with valves and reciprocating piston motion. One of Al-Jazari's humanoid automata was a waitress that could serve water, tea, or drinks. The drink was stored in a tank with a reservoir from where the drink drips into a bucket, and after seven minutes, into a cup, after which the waitress appears out of an automatic door serving the drink. Another was a hand-washing automaton, featuring a female humanoid automaton standing by a basin filled with water. When the user pulls the lever, the water drains, and the female automaton refills the basin. Including a large elephant clock that moved and sounded at the hour, a musical robot band, and a waitress automaton that served drinks, all his works were motivated by the thought of recreating human functions.

The Renaissance witnessed a considerable revival of interest in automata—the technological ingenuity. In 1737, the French engineer, Jacques de Vaucanson, built the world's first biomechanical automaton—The Flute Player. He also constructed another masterpiece, the Digesting Duck, a mechanical duck that gave the false illusion of having the ability to eat kernels of grain, and to metabolise and defecate them. The food was collected in one inner container, and the pre-stored feces was produced from a second container. Another automatons include Wolfgang von

Kempelen's the Turk and the speaking machine. The earlier one consisted of a life-sized model of a human head and torso, with a black beard and grey eyes, and dressed in Ottoman robes and a turban—a mechanism that appeared to play a strong game of chess against a human opponent, as well as perform the knight's tour, a puzzle that requires the player to move a knight to occupy every square of a chessboard exactly once.

When the automatons were creeping up the entertainment history, the interest for humans in sophisticated time-keeping also increased. The initial origins of the time measurement started around 4,000 BC. Another group of thinkers and discoverers emerged as stargazers. They tried to represent the constellations of the stars, pictorially developing the scientific stream of astronomy. The Egyptians even used the astronomical aspects to build the pyramids and the sphinx. The gazers observed the periodic phenomena of appearance of the shooting stars in the sky. Chinese were the masters of such observations. By the second half of the third century BC, the Chinese astronomers had recorded around 300 constellations with a total of 1,164 individual stars in twenty-eight moon houses. In 550 BC, they had built an armillary sphere, a three-dimensional model of heaven, marking the precise positions of stars and heavenly bodies in the sky. There are records of comets and meteorite swarms in the Chinese history, though these records were closely related to the political and religious events. For example, the appearance of the Halley's comet has been recorded in a total of thirty-one times over China in the course of centuries. They also knew the direction of the tail of the comet.

As the astronomy evolved, the scientific community wanted the representation of the sky, the planets, and the constellations in a two-dimensional world. Such instrument was developed by Hipparchus of Nicaea in 160 BC. This instrument did the spatial projection of the sky into a two-dimensional space based on a geocentric model, as known for the mankind at that time. This was the precursor to the Astrolabe developed by Ptolemy later. The astrolabe was finally developed by the Arab scholars who had enthusiasm in the religious foundation. The instrument could determine the direction of Mecca from anywhere around the world, and identify the times of prayer and the dates of Ramadan fasting. Soon in the tenth century, the instrument made its appearance in Western Europe. This instrument is the precursor of the theodolite and the sextant that we used in the modern world for navigation. Without the astrolabe, many of the astronomical discoveries would be impossible, and establishing a relationship between the time and the position would be out of question.

On the other side, the people of Mesopotamia and Assyria gave particular attention to the solar eclipses, and they build specific observatories to gather and assess the information. Their information and the accuracy of prediction surprised the scientists even today. Mostly in Assyria, the solar eclipse was regarded as God's displease on the ruling king, and hence resulted in the death sentence to the ruler. In order to avoid this fate, the king usually used to select a substitute king to represent the true king and accept the death sentence. Once the curse is lifted, the king could come and resume his business as usual. Even today, solar eclipses are considered one of the spectacular natural phenomena, and people are still moved by the mystical effect of solar eclipse.

Throughout the history of mankind, there has been reports of spectacular sightings of comet. It includes the birth of Jesus, the Norman conquest of England, Bayeux tapestry, etc. Even though in 1577 Danish astronomers proved that the sightings are celestial phenomena, it took another 100 years to come out with a theory on its recurrence. It was the astronomer, Edmond Halley, who put forward the theory that comets, like planets, move around the sun in an elliptical orbit and reappeared in a regular basis. He applied the principles of Kepler and Newton to arrive at the frequency of recurrence of the comet that appeared in 1682 as 76.2 years, and concluded that the comet that appeared in 1607, 1531, and 1456 were, in fact, the same comets. He also predicted the appearance of the comet in 1758. He was the first one to establish that the stars that were first considered to be static on the sky actually moved. In respect to the works done by him, the celestial body, which made a frequent visit, was named Halley's comet. Scientists now believe that the nuclei of many of the comets are as old as the solar system, and the research on the clumps of dust and ice of the comets would provide insight into the development of solar system. Halley's comet is due to pass the earth again, as a tribute to the great man, in 2061—if nothing unforeseen happens in the meantime.

Although these observations were made with time as reference, the answer to the question of how to measure time was also solved by the Mesopotamians. They started observing the movement of sun and moon and the shadows they cast. Inspired by the same, they made their first sundial. Since the hexadecimal system had a special meaning for the Babylonians, they divided the entire day into twenty-four hours with each hour of sixty minutes. They developed the first calendar based on the moon phases. But there were discrepancies in their measurement, since the year doesn't consist of whole number of days. Later in 1582, the Pope Gregory XIII introduced the calendar as we see it today. But people were more interested in the immediate time measurement rather the complete year.

Sun was the source of measurement of time as long as there was light. The sundial remained the foundation of communication, planning, and execution till the fourteenth century when the mechanical model clock was invented, although there were some different thoughts in time measurement by the flow of sand, burning of the candle, flow of water through a restriction, etc. By the fourteenth century, the accurate measure of time became inevitable, as Europe was developing as the hub of industry and commercialisation.

The application and the elegance of the automatons were first applied for a practical purpose in the clock-making industry. A mechanism consisting of gears and wheels was developed to show the time by striking a bell. The invention of pendulum increased the accuracy of such set-up considerably, and then the same clocks started to show the time in hour, minute, and seconds. Earlier, there was only one clock in a town, but later miniaturisation enabled everybody to have one with the development of long case clocks, wall, and table clocks. The predecessor of the mechanical clock was first developed by Pacificus in the ninth century. Clockmakers evolved the mechanism of the operation from the pendulum and the weights to the spring drives that made the clocks smaller. Peter Heinlein was the first to make the onion clocks that fitted to the pockets. A real breakthrough came in by the development of the chronometer by John Harrison in 1728. Even on the seafaring ships, his clocks worked well with spring drive. The mechanical clocks and the timepieces reduced the dependency of the man over the nature to sense the time. The time started to govern the human day. This became even more prominent with the invention of the electricity that changed the concept of time measurement. With the advent of electricity, electric power drives could be installed in clocks, and the synchronisation of the number of clocks at the same time was made possible by sending out impulses.

Even though the wristwatches appeared in the nineteenth century, its wider usage began with World War I. By the invention of the quartz crystal oscillation by Morrison in 1929, the 700-year legacy of the mechanical watches and the clocks came to an end. By 1950, when the atomic clock was introduced, it marked the measurement of time with absolute precision.

Anyway, the entertainment automatons, industrialisation, and the concept of time-keeping led to the development of finesse of robotics as we see in the modern world. The term *robot* was first used to denote fictional automata in the 1921 play, *RUR* (*Rossum's Universal Robots*) by the Czech writer, Karel Capek, from the Czech word *robota*, meaning servitude. Many robots were constructed before the dawn of computer-controlled servomechanisms for the public relations purposes of major firms. These were essentially machines that could perform a few stunts like the automatons.

The first humanoid robot was a soldier with a trumpet made in 1810 by Friedrich Kaufmann in Dresden, Germany. The robot was a cardboard cutout connected to various devices, which users could turn on and off. The fully functional robotics was conceptualised by Isaac Asimov who formulated the Three Laws of Robotics; and in the process of doing so, coined the word *robotics*. With Norbert Wiener formulating the principles of cybernetics, practical robotics was born. The first digitally operated and programmable robot was invented by George Devol in 1954 and was ultimately called the Unimate. This ultimately laid the foundations of the modern robotics industry. Devol sold the first Unimate to General Motors in 1960, and it was installed in 1961 in a plant in Trenton, New Jersey to lift hot pieces of metal from a die-casting machine and stack them. Devol's patent for the first digitally operated programmable robotic arm represents the foundation of the modern robotics industry.

The extent to which the robotics has grown is beyond imagination. According to Tractica, the global robotics industry will grow from US$28.3 billion worldwide in 2015 to US$151.7 billion by 2020. Sometime back, I read an article of what we will do in future by Dr Moshe Vardi from Rice University. It was a shock. He expects that within 30 years, machines will be capable of doing almost any job that a human can. We are approaching a time when machines will be able to perform the task that humans used to do in a much more sophisticated manner. As human race, we need to approach this question before it is upon us: if machines are capable of doing any work that humans can do, what will humans do?

A typical answer is that humans will be free to pursue leisure activities. I believe there is an appeal for a leisure-only lifestyle. I believe that for human well-being, he should be occupied. According to the World Economic Forum (WEF), the fourth industrial revolution is transforming the labour markets beyond recognition, leading to a net loss of over five million jobs in fifteen major developed and emerging economies by 2020. WEF estimated that 7.1 million jobs could be lost through redundancy, automation, or disintermediation, while the creation of 2.1 million new jobs mainly in specialised areas such as computing, math, architecture, and engineering. But still, there is a deficiency of five million jobs. Increased leisure time may only become a reality for the underemployed or unemployed. I believe now we can understand why the world is moving to the concept of universal basic income for all. This is a form of social security, which all citizens or residents of a country regularly receive an unconditional sum of money, either from a government or some other public institution, in addition to any income received from elsewhere. So what it will translate to? There will be huge income disparity and social inequality. Inequality between the 1 per cent of the people who hold the wealth and the balance, 99 per cent will widen to an extremely large extend as workforce automation continues.

To give a perspective, a report put out in February 2016 by Citibank, in partnership with the University of Oxford, predicted that 47 per cent of US jobs are at risk of automation. In the UK, 35 per cent are. In China, it's a whopping 77 per cent, while across the OECD it's an average of 57 per cent. And three of the world's ten largest employers, Foxcon, Walmart, and the US Department of Defence, are now replacing their workers with robots.

In a column in The Guardian, the world-famous physicist, Stephen Hawking, wrote that 'the automation of factories has already decimated jobs in traditional manufacturing, and the rise of artificial intelligence is likely to extend this job destruction deep into the middle classes with only the most caring, creative, or supervisory roles remaining'. 'Automation will, in turn, accelerate the already widening economic inequality around the world,' Hawking wrote. 'The Internet and the platforms that it makes possible allow very small groups of individuals to make enormous profits while employing very few people. This is inevitable, it is progress, but it is also socially destructive.'

Combined with other issues—overpopulation, climate change, diseases—we are, Hawking warns ominously, at 'the most dangerous moment in the development of humanity'. Humanity must come together if we are to overcome these challenges, he says. It is a moment of realisation.

To accept what is going to be our future, Adam Keiper, the editor of The New Atlantis, a Journal on Technology and Society, describes possible three scenarios that could reflect the future of automation. Automation and artificial intelligence will continue to advance, but at a pace sufficiently slower that society and the economy can gradually absorb the changes, so that people can take advantage of the new possibilities without suffering the most disruptive effects. The job market will change, but in something like the way it has evolved over the last half-century: some kinds of jobs will disappear, but new kinds of jobs will be created, and by and large people will be able to adapt to the shifting demands on them while enjoying the great benefits that automation makes possible.

In the second scenario, automation, robotics, and artificial intelligence will advance very rapidly. Jobs will disappear at a pace that will make it difficult for the workforce to adapt without widespread pain. The kinds of jobs that will be threatened will increasingly be jobs that had been relatively immune to automation—the high-skilled jobs that generally involved creativity and problem-solving, and the low-skilled jobs that involved manual dexterity or some degree of adaptability and interpersonal relations. The pressures on low-skilled workers will exacerbate the pressures already felt because of competition from low-paid workers. Among the disappearing jobs may be those at the lower-wage end of the spectrum that we have counted on for decades to instill basic workplace skills and values in our young people, and that have served as a kind of employment safety net for older people transitioning in their lives. And the balance between labour and capital may (at least for a time) shift sharply in favour of capital, as the share of gross domestic product (GDP) that flows to the owners of physical capital (e.g., the owners of artificial intelligences and robots) rises and the share of GDP that goes to workers falls. If this scenario unfolds quickly, it could involve severe economic disruption, perhaps social unrest, and maybe calls for political reform.

In the third scenario, advances in automation, robotics, and artificial intelligence will produce something utterly new. Even within this scenario, the range of possibilities is vast. Perhaps we will see the creation of emulations—minds that have been uploaded into computers. Perhaps we will see the rise of powerful artificial superintelligences, unpredictable and dangerous. Perhaps we will reach a 'singularity' moment after which everything that matters most will be different from what came before. These types of possibilities are increasingly matters of discussion for technologists, but their very radicalness makes it difficult to say much about what they might mean at a human scale, except insofar as they might involve the extinction of humanity as we know it. This scenario of consciousness emerging from AI is forecasted by Elon Musk and Stephen Hawking as a terminator being born, as we had discussed earlier. We have to wait and see what would emerge.

9

ARE WE CHANGING MASLOW'S HIERARCHY OF EARTH?

I felt lost when I woke up. Did I drink so much to get such a hang over? No, never. I was on the way back from my office in the crowded lanes of Powai. I was irritated with the discussions that I had in the office. These guys do not even listen to what I am saying. I made a big mistake by making the decision to join this firm. I think I should go and clear the steam out. The company has already making me diffident on the topic that I had been working for over ten years. But anyway, why should I argue? It would waste my time and my energy. I'd rather call my friend Arya. She was my classmate, no strings attached. Could rely on her for being a good listen to whatever shit I say.

I made the booking for me and Arya at Engima in Andheri. Around 7 p.m., we met up outside the lounge. She was dressed casually, the way I was, and I really wanted to cool my head off— not yet for the party.

Arya was a psychiatrist by profession. She was always a good company whenever I got irritated. She had a husband who was also a psychiatrist. We all were a good company since we started going for treks together. Anyway, the good part was that I could say anything to her. We got to a corner, and she ordered a pitcher of beer for both of us. The music was just climbing the pitch, and our discussion was getting heated. We discussed various topics about the family and the company. The heat of discussion climbed, and

JOSEPH ANTONY PULIKKOTTIL

I could count the glasses of beer I had. She started putting up the topic of Maslow's hierarchy on the table. Even though I knew about the hierarchy, she defined it more in a psychiatric way.

'I believe that every person has a strong desire to realise his or her full potential to reach a level of self-actualisation. The main point of this prioritisation is to enhance the positive potential of human beings. You must understand that.'

'What the hell is happening to my life? Have I not made any priorities in life?'

'Joe, you must be clear what you need to do. No point in blaming someone for you not doing something that you want.'

'I completely agree with you, Arya. I will try once my head is okay.'

'Oh my god, where am I? Arya, am I at your home?'

'Joe, it is already eleven. I think you knocked off yesterday, and Arya brought you here.' It was Shyam, Arya's husband.

'Oh, dude, am really sorry.'

'No problem, Joe. Anyway, we wanted to meet you after a long time. Let us have brunch.'

I had English-style brunch with omelettes, sausages, and bacon, all stuffed with brown bread and Earl Grey tea—awesome.

I thanked Arya and Shyam and booked an Uber back home. I was in the car and started to learn more about the hierarchy that include his observations of humans' innate curiosity. The hierarchy is a pyramid with the largest, most fundamental levels of needs at the bottom, and the need for self-actualisation and self-transcendence at the top. Yes, I got my topic of interest, the self-actualisation, but it is the top portion of the hierarchy. What is at the bottom, which I need to worry? Air and water are the fundamental requirements for human and for all the living organisms. These fundamental requirements will translate into food into metabolic requirements too for all the organisms. For the evolved creations, such as human, in the Maslow's hierarchy, then comes the clothing and shelter that would provide necessary protection. Obviously, another fundamental need would be the human sexual instinct and competition that would shape the said instinct. So fundamentally, for my self-actualisation, we should start from the bottom portion of the Maslow's pyramid. Do we currently have such fundamental requirements, and will we continue to have these requirements satisfied for our future generations through the resources that are available on earth?

Before describing the hierarchy of earth, which I thought of doing after hearing from Arya, once in a while I used to wonder how small our earth is and human as part of the universe. I used to wonder how our galaxy got the name the Milky Way. In my school, I could gather that the name came since it looked very attractive when looked through a telescope, and it is white in colour. After going through the Greek mythology, I was wonderstruck with a creative story we had imagined and framed. Zeus's son, Hercules, was suckling the breasts of the goddess, Hera, when she was sleeping. Zeus wanted Hercules to suck in immortality along with her milk. But accidentally, Hercules had a burp, and some milk was split and became a luminous band of light in the sky. The Milky Way is this split milk.

But soon, the creative story gave way to objective reasoning. The Greek philosophers suggested that this white nebula is nothing but a mass of separate stars, and Galileo proved the same through his telescope. But it was the Englishman, Thomas Wright, who brought in some order to the way and its stars. He claimed that it is not a way, but a group of several planetary systems in the shape of a disc. He published his learning through his work, *An Original Theory and New Hypothesis of the Universe*. Inspired by this work, Immanuel Kant developed his own ideas on the structure and origin of the universe. Kant took a remarkable step beyond Wright by concluding that the Milky Way was one among the many stellar systems existing in the universe. He also discovered similar galaxies existing, which are now known as Orion and Andromeda. He concluded that all these systems shared some common properties such as its shape and the style of rotation. In order to support his postulates, he used Newton and Kepler's laws of gravity and planetary motion.

Instead of seeing the whole universe as the result of a divine act, Kant explained the origin through the laws of natural science. Although Kant is admired for his visionary power, many of the ideas of Kant and Wright were confirmed later by astronomers using improved equipment. But one of the most debated topic ever in the history of mankind remained whether the sun moved around the earth, or the earth moved around the sun. Although the concept of Heliocentricity was first proposed by Aristotle way back in 350 BC, Aristarchus of Samos in 280 BC was the first to demonstrate the same. Based on his calculations of the distances between the earth, moon, the sun, and their relative sizes, Aristarchus also recognised that the earth once rotated on its own axis once a day, while the sun and other stars remain immovable. He also estimated the distance of sun was twenty times more than the distance of moon from Earth. Even though, according to the new estimates, his observations were far lower, but at his times, these views were out of the box. Moreover, his contemporaries accused him for disregarding the religious laws of the time.

Even with the knowledge of the work of Aristarchus, Ptolemy in 150BC was a strong proposer of the geocentric model. It was only in the about AD 1500 that Nicholas Copernicus refuted Ptolemy's concept and recognised the Heliocentric model, which thereby solved a lot of astronomical problems. It was a revolutionary opinion of science in history, and the Catholic church did not even accept the principle for centuries. It is quite amazing how Copernicus discovered the Heliocentric model. After he completed his law graduation, he started working in an observatory in Prussia where he could observe that moon was covering up the star, Aldebaran. This made him think about the validity of geocentric model.

Although the Ptolemy's geocentric model was widely accepted in those days, there was a significant drawback on that theory. The calendar calculations based the geocentric theory was coming incorrect. It was then Copernicus came across the theory of Aristarchus on heliocentricity. He worked on the same and came up with his main work, *De Revolutionibus Orbium Coelestrium* (On the Revolution of Celestial Bodies), which came into light only after his death. Inspired by him, his work was completed by Galileo Galilee. It took centuries for the theologians to accept the theory that rejected the hypothesis that the earth was the centre of universe. The Catholic church accepted the theory of Copernicus only in 1996. But there was a theology student who became interested in the new view of world postulated by Copernicus. It was none other than Johannes Kepler. In his work published in 1596, he formulated the theory that the sun exerts pull on its planets, and that keep them moving in circular orbits. In 1600, he moved to Prague and met Tycho Brahe who had an immense collection of data on the movements of planets.

With the death of the Brahe, Kepler became the mathematician and the astronomer of the imperial court of Bohemia, Hungary. With the help of information he received from Brahe, he arrived at the remarkable conclusion that the planets do not travel in circular orbits, but rather elliptical orbits. He also notices that the planets move faster when they are near the sun, and slower when away from the sun. It was during this time that he derived the theory of planetary motion and came out with his laws. It is believed that Isaac Newton derived his theory of gravity from these laws, and used them to estimate the mass of planets from the distances and the orbital periods of their moons. For the first time, the Kepler's laws gave a realistic model of the solar system, and as a decisive proof for the validity of the Copernican hypothesis.

As we know today, Newton discovered the gravity after an apple fell on his head. But it was not Newton who came with the concept of gravity. Aristotle, around 370 BC, had proposed that a body would fall faster if it is heavier and slower if it is lighter. This concept was maintained for hundreds of years till the Dutch mathematician, Simon Stevin, proved that despite the difference in weights, the time taken by two balls are identical. Though he couldn't prove with a theory, the proposal was sensational during his times. Later, Galileo took this challenge. But the primary obstacle he had to face was the speed of the fall was so fast that he couldn't measure the time with the clocks that were available then. He moved his experiment to an inclined plane, so that he could measure the time of the falling ball accurately with a water clock. Then he devised an apparatus to test the same on the leaning tower of Pisa— the well-known experiment of all times. He was trying to prove that the despite of the angle of inclination of the fall, the final speed of the falling objects would be the same. He achieved the same with the help of the pendulum. He noted the same while watching the swinging of the candelabrum of the Pisa Cathedral, and came to the conclusion that the period of pendulum oscillation was independent of the swing or the weight of the pendulum. This was a landmark observation that led to the laws of gravity. Thus, the Aristotelian spell was broken and paved the way to the modern physics.

It was around this time that the apple fell. It was not just the definition of gravity that originated in the great mind; it also defined the laws of nature that governed our everyday lives. The close association of Newton with Edmund Halley, who was the professor of geometry at the university of Oxford, fascinated Newton to take up the concept of universal gravity to explain the planetary motion. Starting from the premise that there must be a fundamental force of attraction between the sun and the planets to maintain the balance of the system, he started to study on the interaction of the bodies, and thus on the principles of motion. On the basis of Kepler's laws of planetary motion, which accepted that there was a force of attraction between themselves as well as the force of attraction of the sun, Newton formulated the three laws of motion. This marked the beginning of a completely new science—the dynamics. He also formulated the law of universal gravitation in which he postulated the force of mutual attraction depends on the mass of the bodies and their distance apart. For small objects, this force may be negligible; but for the astronomical objects, such as planets, there would be a significant effect on the related bodies. He published his findings in 1687, much before the nuclear and electromagnetic forces were identified, through his book, *The Mathematical Principles of Natural Philosophy*.' The idea that everybody in the universe attracted each other remained the foundation of scientific conception for another 200 years. Then came the idea of nothingness, which even Aristotle feared a perfect vacuum, complete emptiness of matter.

The early works and investigations of vacuum have paved the way to many interesting discoveries of air pressure. The initial thoughts on the vacuum concept arose at the time of reformation. In an experiment in 1644, a physicist, Evangelista Torricelli, inverted a glass tube sealed in one end and filled with mercury into a tumbler that contained mercury, leaving behind an empty space in the tube when the level of the mercury sank. This experiment raised a heated debate in the learned community, as all of them believed that the space created was ether. The sentiment of the community could be well understood from the comment that Blaise Pascal made: 'Nature would rather face her own demise than the smallest empty space.'

The discord among the community continued till Otto Guericke, a German enthusiast, invented a pump to suck out air from enclosed containers. With the help of the same, he demonstrated the famous experiment of Magdeburg hemispheres in Regensburg, Germany. He attached two hemispheres and pumped out air from within and used eight horses in vain to pull them apart, proving the existence and power of vacuum. The observation of Guericke was not accepted, since the postulate was against the popular belief that a medium ether was required for the carriage of light waves. It was later in the twentieth century that the traditional ideas of space began to change.

The concept of matter and space was in place. It was the Greeks that took these natural sciences to the next level. It was not just their mathematical skills that differentiated them from those in Egypt and Mesopotamia. They tried to work out the logical proofs for the laws they considered as the laws of nature. There was a field that was emerging as the natural science during the campaigns of Alexander the Great around 330 BC. Theophrastus of Eresus, a student of Aristotle, prepared the botanical specimens of Alexander's campaigns in which he made many ethnological and scientific observations on the customs of people, geography, plants, animals, and the minerals found. Similar to Aristotle, who gave zoology a scientific base, Theophrastus gave the same to the botany. *Historia Plantarum* that he wrote in 300 BC is considered to be one of the finest books ever existed on the topic at that time, and it was based on this book that the modern botanical studies and the classifications were made by Leonhart Fuchs.

This is the extreme short story of Earth and its characteristics, as we know today. But how did we learn about these characteristics? We started with the Greek mathematician, Euclid, who created the systematic theory of analysing the shapes of nature. His treatise that consists of thirteen volume compendiums became the most influential book till date, and the complete treatise of the mathematical knowledge till his times. Alongside the geometry, he also formulated the concept of prime number. His ideas of the geometry were not questioned till Nikolai Lobachevsky founded the non-Euclidian geometry, which found application at the beginning of the twentieth century in the theory of relativity. But for around 2,200 years after the Euclidian geometry was formed, the measurement of the flat earth was completely dependent on his formulations.

On the other side of the geometry lies the complex figure of perfecting the circle. From the fifth century BC, it was known that the area of circle was always in proportion to the square of the radius of the circle. But the constant ratio at which the area varies was still a dilemma. The first person to tackle this issue was Archimedes in 250 BC. He explained that if a polygon was drawn inside and outside of a circle, then the area of the circle would be half the areas of both the polygons—the larger the number of angles of the figure, the better the accuracy for the constant pi. From the hexagon, he drew polygon with ninety-six sides, and with each increase of the sides of the polygon, the diagram became closer to circle and he finally arrived at a conclusion that the value of pi is between 3 10/70 and 3 10/71. This was a major step in conquering the complexity of the circle. Later in AD 263, Liu Hui in China went a step ahead and constructed a polygon with 3,072 angles, and he derived a much more accurate value of pi to 3.14159. Even though after the introduction of concept of infinity and irrational numbers in mathematics and the super computers for calculation, the value of pi still remains inaccurate.

Our leap on earth sciences was based on the principles of observation, and mathematics formed the theory behind all sciences. On one hand, it is the practical application, and on the other it is the principle of observation. As a discipline and a methodology, mathematics had its origins by the Egyptians, Babylonians, and the Mayans for astronomical purposes and for surveying land. But it was during the period of awakening in Greece when the philosophy opened up space for abstract thought. It was Pythagoras who showed the illumination of a scientific approach. His work was mainly in geometry, and his theorem that he developed in 500 BC is world famous. Following Pythagoras, Euclid started developing theories that opened up the concept of Euclidian geometry. His thoughts made early contribution to systematic building of mathematical rules. People and the scholars were equally enthusiastic about the new thought and, soon, his work.

Elements became one of the most read books ever in line with Bible. The geometry had such an importance in the life of Greeks that any scholar who wanted to join an elite learning club had to be the master of geometry, since the Greek used geometry to solve the problems in algebra to trigonometry using the principle of Euclidian geometry. Not for nothing did the inscription over the portal of Plato's academy read, 'Do not enter those who are unacquainted with geometry.'

On the other hand, in India, though people were working on mathematics from around 1,000 BC, they started the algebrasation of mathematics around AD 500. In the discussion of the development of mathematics, no word goes without the invention of zero. The known case of the usage of zero was in Babylon in about 300 BC, since they already had a system of place values (for 123, 1 was place in hundreds column, 2 was placed in tens column, and 3 in the units or the last column). When the place value was missing, they used the sign of a slanting double wedge to join the two numbers, so that all the numbers could be placed in its correct place without ambiguity. This was a decisive moment in the promotion of accuracy.

In the Mayan civilisation, the use of zero was popular. They used a glyph a pictorial character. It was the Alexander who introduced the Babylonian ideas in India, and zero received a status in India. During the second century AD, Indians had an evolved system of arithmetic, geometry, and algebra. In AD 500, Indians had a decimal system with a perfect value system. Around AD 600, Brahmagupta has been using the negative numbers in his calculations. The symbol, zero, appears for the first time in AD 876 in a temple inscription in Gwalior. The symbol zero opened up a completely new dimension in the understanding of mathematics.

Further development in the field of mathematics was carried out by the Arabs. They took the same numbers, and the place values used by Indians, and further developed algebra. The term Algebra itself is taken from the book by Al Kwarizmi, which also mentions the word algorithm. It took a long time for the mathematical thoughts to sprout into the western world. What did we do with the knowledge that we had acquired through the experiments and observation? We passed on through the next generation through various modes of communication.

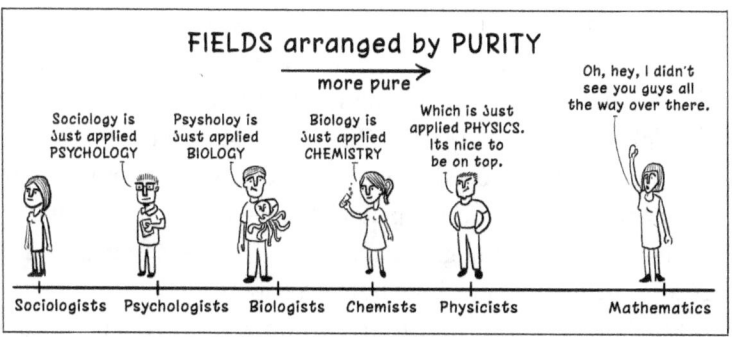

FIELDS arranged by PURITY

more pure →

Sociology is Just applied PSYCHOLOGY

Psysholoy is Just applied BIOLOGY

Biology is Just applied CHEMISTRY

Which is Just applied PHYSICS. Its nice to be on top.

Oh, hey, I didn't see you guys all the way over there.

Sociologists Psychologists Biologists Chemists Physicists Mathematics

When the world was advancing, the desire for communication becomes a discussion of prime consideration. Passing on the knowledge accumulated in course of time is one of the oldest traditions of human kind. Since the oral transmission couldn't preserve the cultural heritage forever, man relied on lifelike representation and vivid graphic symbols to represent this ideas or events.

Later, a complex cuneiform (wedge-shaped) script was developed in southern Mesopotamia and Sumeria in 4000 BC. It was written on clay tablets using a spatula-shaped tool. The tablets were fired to make them more durable. Slowly, the phonetics started to be used in a standard form, and the same evolved. Egyptian were the first to standardise the language under the hieroglyphs around 3,000 BC, which meant holy signs, since they believed that it was invented by the God, Thot. As far as the pictorial language is concerned, the Chinese script survives the test of times. It has developed from a pictorial to a word script retaining its original form even today. The languages like the Korean, the Japanese, and almost all of the East Asian languages have a common thread to associate to the Chinese script.

How did the western alphabet originate? The Roman alphabet has twenty-six characters, unlike the hieroglyphs of 800 odd characters and Chinese is 6,000–8,000 characters. All the alphabets have a common origin and can be traced back to North Semitic character script, which contains only consonants used around 1,500 BC. The Greeks started to use the same by adding vowels to make their alphabet in eighth century BC. The Phoenicians who lived in the Asia Minor developed a simple and different script based on consonants compared to the pictorial language of the Egyptians. This language was brought to the Greece by the merchants, and was also the basis of the first Greek alphabets.

But how did the basic desire of the man to communicate evolve? Its development had started even before the origin of the scripts. Indian used smoke, Africans the drums, and the Romans the torches to transmit the information acoustically or visually. In around 1,500 BC, the Persians, Greeks, and the Romans used messengers to deliver oral messages. In 27 BC, the landmark system of postal effort was started by Augustus by setting up a network of mail coaches. By fifteenth century, the network evolved into a real postal service, increasing the literary communication not just within the limit the church and the authorities but also among the common man.

The printing also contributed significantly to the evolution of communication, but the real impact came after the invention of the electricity, which led to the development of Morse code by Samuel Morse transforming the time for information dissemination from days to hours. The new era in the communication came with the arrival of telephone by Alexander Graham Bell in 1876. People felt much closer than ever before as the chat over the phone expressed one's feelings in addition to the words.

By the end of twentieth century, the mass media communication revolutionised the world through the radio, TV, and films. With the arrival of these mediums, the one-way interaction started to be accepted among people. The first radio broadcast when started in 1924, there were hardly any audience, but by the end of 1925, there were a million users on this medium. The growth of television also saw too quick reception in the world and became indispensable part of any home.

When the basic needs getting satisfied with these innovations, the intellectual needs stimulated man to think about the social organisations. The concept of state and the country was getting developed, and the state bureaucracy and the controls started to get stronger. The busy administrative machinery needed the support of documentation that led to the invention of a medium to write. Around 4,000 BC, Mesopotamians used the soft wooded sheets to write. Around the same time, the Egyptians started to use the papyrus as their medium of writing. Even though the paper was invented in China in AD 105, it was guarded as a state secret, and hence the technology took more than 1,000 years to get to Spain, Germany, and Italy where the technology developed to the way we see now. If the papyrus has not inspired the Egyptians to make the paper, the period from 4,000 BC to the Middle Ages, when the Chinese invented the technique, would have been an era of unrecorded cultural history.

In parallel, the Egyptians and the Chinese introduced the ink with the sesame oil and the soot. The usage of the script, the paper, the ink, and its understanding was limited to the elite in the social strata who held powerful positions in the administration and government of the country. Professional clerks and copyists spend their entire lives in copying books. The invention of movable metal type by Gutenberg in 1445 revolutionised the process of multiplication of books. There were individual characters that were arranged to form a block of words, and thus sentences from which the printed impressions could be taken. The reuse of the charters cast in the standard sizes resulted in the speedier reproduction of books. The printing, thus, was more objective than handwritten copies of books, and was prone to less mistakes.

The discovery enabled the scholars to study scientific works and literature. Between 1452 and 1454, Gutenberg printed the 180 copies of forty-two-line Gutenberg bible. A number of mechanical devices appeared subsequently to facilitate writing. In 1714, Henry Mill patented the writing machine as a precursor to the typewriter. Mark Twain was the first writer to send a manuscript to the publisher by keeping the original with him, since he himself had a typewriter. The basic principle of the Gutenberg's printing remained till the twentieth century when the mechanical type setting machines succeeded from the technique of film setting in 1946.

Anyway, the discovery of the printing press contributed to the general education of the population, and undoubtedly contributed enormously to the development of the mankind. The key reason for the dormancy of innovation was the apocalyptic Christian atmosphere that didn't support innovation. In AD 1,200, Leonardo of Pisa set up the first European memorial to the new Arabic numeral, which arrived in Europe. As the trade started to progress, the methods of solving the basic mathematical operations—the addition, subtraction, the multiplication, and the division—started to be used by the fifteenth century. Soon, with the arrival of the Gutenberg press, scholars started to publish comprehensive books on mathematics, and the most popular to come up was Adam Reisse in 1530s. These books led to the popular saying according to Adam Reise.

By 1550s, even the decimal system started to be established. During the same time, a standardised system of symbols gained more favour. Instead of writing in the normal way, people started using symbols. The pace of innovative thoughts raced by the invention of logarithms. This enabled us to use addition and subtraction to work out larger numbers, which otherwise were never heard of. People started to use the words of hundreds, thousands, and ten thousand. These advances increased the capabilities of mathematics. By the seventeenth century, the creation of analytical geometry enabled the solution of geometry problems by algebraic operations resulting in the developments of work by Fermat and Descartes. Through the groundbreaking work, *Discourse of Method* by Descartes, he solved the long-standing problem of combining geometry with algebra. In this work, which was collection of three excerpts from his work, *Le Monde* (The World), he established the foundation of modern mathematics through the coordinate geometry. This key concept enabled the mathematicians to describe the Euclidian three-dimensional and two-dimensional space into equations and solve the same. They could use the Cartesian coordinates to construct and project the objects and points in three dimension numerically. He described the plane to X, Y, and Z coordinates. Through this treatment of geometry analytically, any dimensions could be added in the space. This breakthrough thought from the mind, which had the philosophy 'Cogito ergo sum', meaning I think therefore I am, was the foundation of modern rationalism and became a decisive factor in the Einstein's theory of relativity, and further development of the functions and calculus.

During the period of enlightenment, Newton and Leibniz developed the concept of calculus, which, in a way, paved the way to the concept of infinity. Suddenly, the abstract functions could be easily captured by the mathematical functions of calculus and limits. Following the ways of Newton, Euler developed the analytical models for angle functions, exponentials, and logarithms, revolutionising the world of science.

Today, the mathematical works of Descartes, Leibniz, and Newton have found their way into everybody's work and leisure by means of computer graphics and virtual reality. Even though the development of most of the streams in natural sciences can be attributed to structural thinking of man, there are a few exceptions. The discovery of probability theory is one among them. In 1650, a gambler and a writer, Antonie Chevalier de Mere, questioned the French mathematician, Pascal, about the outcome of a bet. How often was it possible to throw a double six with two dice, throwing dice several times? Pascal responded out of six times six (i.e., out of thirty-six times) only once would there be an occurrence of double six. He was satisfied, but came out with another question, which was, in fact, more difficult to answer. How should the players in the game divide the pool when they break up the pool and then decide to break up the game prematurely? The money should be divided according to the winning chances of individual players at the time of break-up.

In 1654, de Mere discussed this problem with Fermat in an extensive correspondence, marking the beginning of the methodical probability theory. Later in the seventeenth century, the Swiss mathematician, Jakob Bernoulli, published the work *The Art of Conjecturing or Speculating*, providing a systematic foundation to the study of probability. He tried to assess the cogency of an argument based on the degree of certainty. He also put forward the theory of large numbers in which he postulated the convergence of mathematical probability and the actual frequency of occurrence, if the experiment was carried out more number of times. Today, this law is the foundation of probability. As the insurance business developed in the nineteenth century, the probability heaped to assess the risk against the people who were insured. Without probability, the world we know of today will be hard to imagine.

There were some crucial advances around this time in which there was a huge interest in improved instruments for calculations. As the various fields of sciences started venturing into unchartered waters, the computational needs also started to pile up. In addition, the flourishing of international trade made the measurement, counting, and arithmetic important than even before. Taking the inputs from the abacus invented earlier, John Napier invented the Napier bones, which solved the problem of counting.

The community also started using slide rule as a way for measurement. In 1623, Wilhelm Schickard came out with the first effort to mechanise the basic arithmetical processes of addition, subtraction, multiplication, and division using the clockwork principle. Six ten-tooth wheels for six digits were connected and the user could read the values from 0 to 9, while each wheel rotated through ten positions and 360 degrees. Each wheel was geared to the other wheel, and became the first mechanical effort of the mankind to automate the calculations. Later a number of mathematicians followed the principle and constructed one. They include Blaise Pascal and Leibniz who presented a living calculator the Royal society.

There was a distinct feature on the mechanical calculator presented by Leibniz. This was a predecessor of the modern computer, since it worked on binary system. It was he who introduced man to the binary system of representation by describing one a godly number and other the devilish number, which later go translated to true and false in the computer age. In 1679, when Leibniz published this binary system, he also mentioned the method to do basic operators on these numbers. He represented the seven days of godly creation as 111, which don't include a devilish character. Although he proposed the use of binary system, for the conversion of heathens in vain, the system became extremely prominent in other areas, preparing the way for modern electronic data processing.

Since the ideas generated, developed, and passed on through earlier generations, human beings evolved and with the rapid movement from Homo sapiens to Homo economicus (a term that describes the rational human being assumed by some economists when deriving, explaining, and verifying theories and models).

There had been a huge impact on the Maslow's hierarchy. But what did we do with this knowledge and understanding about the universe? We almost gave a direct hit the Maslow's hierarchy of earth. Starting with the industrial revolution, with the increasing use of fossil fuels, we are increasing the warmth of planet earth and pushing Mother Nature to a new territory at a rate that she had never seen before. Average temperature has increased by 1.7 degrees since 1880, which may not seem large, but the heat of emissions by human activity is equivalent of 400,000 Hiroshima bombs across the world every single day. The future generations are in big trouble, and the earth will gradually continue to get warmer and storms will grow more intense and draughts longer in tenure. If the emissions continue to rise unchecked, the process will destabilise entire nation send millions of refugees across borders cause widespread extinction of most species on earth and melt polar ice caps, making most of the coastal cities sink several feet underwater. All this could take centuries, but something like sudden collapse of agriculture trigger immediate chaos in the society.

Best case is we get our act together and begin to rapidly bring emission levels down, and meanwhile, earth turns out to be less sensitive to greenhouse gases than we currently believe, plants and animals adapt quickly, and major technological breakthroughs help society limit emissions and adjust to climate change. But these are all the opposite of what actually seems. The only thing in our control is to limit the missions using all available tools and best behaviours currently at our disposal. Worst case collapse in production causes spiralling prices and is our capitalist utopia breaks down, and billions starve as our world gets violent and messy like a zombie apocalypse. This will be coupled with the abandoning of many of our greatest cities, and the worst part would be the majority of the greenhouse emissions had been done building these metropolises. If the emissions continue unchecked, we're looking at a total rise of between 80 and 160 feet, and the question is how fast scientists expect this to happen?

The past data suggest that it would occur at a rate of one foot per decade, which would result in we giving up the current coastlines to new ones. But only the computer forecasts give us a range of future possibilities, but most important evidence comes from the study of past climate conditions, which clearly show that every time the amount of carbon dioxide rises, the earth warms up. We are in uncharted territory. Humans have been pumping carbon dioxide much more than time in the history of the earth.

To give a general perception of pollution, according to WHO, ambient air pollution contributes to 6.7 per cent of all deaths worldwide. About seven million premature deaths annually are linked to air pollution, according to WHO. That is one in eight deaths worldwide. As we live every day through everything we do, we leave greenhouse gases, the carbon dioxide, methane, and the nitrous oxide (the laughing gas), which is referred as the carbon footprint. The main source of CO_2 is the burning of fossil fuels and methane is the decomposition of organic matter in the absence of oxygen. Methane is produced in the green fields where our crops are manured and even from the digestive tracts of cows and sheep, which is emitted to the atmosphere. The nitrous oxide is formed when bacteria decomposes nitrogen compounds.

Among the culprits, methane is a powerful global warming pollutant, at least twenty-five times more potent than carbon dioxide. More than one-third of all US methane emissions are a result of methane from the oil and gas industry. Oil and gas companies can reduce industry's harmful methane emissions by 80 per cent and generate US$2 billion annually simply by fixing leaks, according to a report released by the Natural Resources Defence Council. These cost-effective actions would cut total US methane emissions by approximately one-third, which is equivalent to the global warming pollution from more than fifty coal-fired power plants. More than 80 per cent of people in urban areas are exposed to air quality levels that exceed World Health Organization limits. As urban air quality declines, the risk of diseases, such as strokes, heart disease, lung cancer, and asthma, goes up. Outdoor air pollution could cost the world a whopping US$2.6 trillion a year or 1 per cent of global GDP, nine million premature deaths by 2060, says the study by the Organization for Economic Cooperation and Development. The costs are a result of sick days, medical bills, and reduced agricultural output. China, Russia, and India would be the worst affected ones. Welfare costs associated with these deadly consequences are projected to rise to as much as US$25 trillion over the same period. The amount associated with paying for the pain and suffering from illness is estimated to hit US$2.2 trillion.

By the way, air pollution is not just a case of today. Back in the Middle Ages, the use of coal in cities such as London was beginning to escalate. By the thirteenth century, coal mining was well established in the North East, and coal was shipped to London as an alternative fuel to wood. Air pollution began to be noticeable, and people began to feel unwell. Some tried to restrict the use of coal. The problems of poor urban air quality caused by coal being burned for domestic heating and industry are well-documented even as early as the end of the sixteenth century. Charles II, the king of England, Scotland, and Ireland, commissioned the scientist, John Evelyn, to make a study of the effects of coal smoke on health, plant life, and buildings. He published *Fumifugium* or the *Inconveniencie of the Aer and Smoak of London Dissipated* in 1661, the first complete study of air pollution, which described the details of the problem, proposed solutions by recommending the relocation of the coal plants from the city centre, and increased planting of flora in the city of London.

With the arrival of industrialisation in eighteenth and nineteenth century, the use of coal was not just in the households. It started to be used for steam power and gas production, creating even more pollution. In the nineteenth Century, regulations were introduced to start to tackle air pollution. In 1863 and 1874, the Alkali Act was brought in to control pollution from chemical works. In December 1952, London was affected by a severe smog that lasted five days. It was estimated that there were at least 4,000 additional deaths as a result of the smog, including a ninefold increase in deaths from bronchitis.

The Clean Air Act of 1956 was the first serious attempt to deal with air pollution from domestic sources, and which introduced the concept of smoke control areas. In 1961, the UK established the world's first coordinated national air pollution monitoring network called the National Survey. In 1990, the Environmental Protection Act replaced the Alkali Act to become the authority for waste management and control of emissions into the environment. Globally, there came the cap on the emissions of benzene, 1, 3-butadiene, carbon monoxide, lead, NO_2, ozone, PM10, and SO_2, and then started the curbing of pollution on the most polluting economy—the transport economy. In the outdoors, despite the common air pollutants, which affect ambient air quality that include sulphur dioxide, nitrogen oxides, carbon monoxide, particulate matter, and volatile organic compounds (VOCs), emitted through the burning of fossil fuels for energy and transportation, ozone, a secondary pollutant, is also formed near ground level when primary pollutants are oxidised in the presence of sunlight. The resulting cocktail of pollution can have detrimental effects on human health, wildlife, and vegetation. Asthma is an increasingly common respiratory disease, which may be triggered by air pollution. In addition, sulphur dioxide and nitrogen oxides may be converted into acids and deposited as acid rain.

Indoors, poor ventilation can lead to a build-up of air pollutants including carbon monoxide and nitrogen dioxide from faulty gas heaters and cookers, carbon monoxide and benzene from cigarette smoke, and VOCs from synthetic furnishings, vinyl flooring, and paints. Like outdoor pollutants, indoor pollutants may also act as triggers for attacks of asthma. Since most of us spend up to 90 per cent of the time indoors, indoor air quality could have a real bearing on our health.

Despite the traditional techniques to tackle air pollution, including lower emission vehicles (including electric, hybrid, and LPG), car sharing, and lower emission sources of heat and power, there are a few technologies showing surprising leaps of faith. One among them is the Gas to Liquids solution. GTL is the umbrella term for the technology that is used to produce a suite of synthetic hydrocarbon liquids through the Fischer-Tropsch process. The GTL process consists of three stages. In the first stage, natural gas is partially oxidised to create a mixture of hydrogen and carbon monoxide, which is then known as synthesis gas or syngas. Impurities are removed from the syngas. The second stage converts the synthesis gas into liquid hydrocarbons using a catalyst. In this stage, a liquid is formed, which looks and feels like wax at room temperature. The final stage is cracking and isomerisation, which cuts the molecule chains into shorter lengths. This yields high-quality liquids such as diesel, kerosene, and lubricant oil. Shell has been pioneer in the GTL technology and has opened the world's first commercial GTL plant in Bintulu, Malaysia in 1993.

The World Bank estimates that over 150 billion cubic metres of natural gas are flared or vented annually, an amount worth approximately US$30.6 billion, equivalent to 25 per cent of the United States' gas consumption, or 30 per cent of the European Union's annual gas consumption. This can work as a resource that could be useful using GTL. Gas-to-liquid processes may also be used for the economic extraction of gas deposits in locations where it is not economical to build a pipeline. This process will be increasingly significant as crude oil resources are depleted.

Another technology that could be coming up in future on is the hydrogen fuel enhancement, a process of using a mixture of hydrogen and conventional hydrocarbon fuel in an internal combustion engine. Methods for such a technology would include hydrogen produced through electrolysis, stored as a second fuel, or aiding effective burning of conventional fuel with hydrogen as a catalyst. The driverless cars are also expected to improve fuel efficiency by 15–40 per cent, reducing emissions of local pollutants, as well as greenhouse gases.

Another breakthrough is done by the technology company, Dearman. It is developing an alternative system based on the use of 'liquid air', which produces zero emissions on the road. The engine is a novel piston engine driven by the expansion of liquid nitrogen to produce clean cold and power. The concept that the company uses is that liquid nitrogen expands 710 times between liquid and gas phases. They operate like high-pressure steam engines, but the difference is that the boiling liquid is not water but nitrogen. The low-boiling temperature of liquid nitrogen eliminates the need for a traditional fuel. The only emission from a Dearman engine is air or nitrogen with no emissions of NO_x, CO_2, or particulates.

Though these technologies are controlling the emissions on the source, there are technologies that have emerged to work on removing the pollution particles that are mostly made up of carbon. Dutch designer, Daan Roosegaarde, and his team of experts have created the world's largest smog vacuum cleaner, Smog Free Tower, an air-purifying tower, which sucks in pollution and expels clean air. The device is a twenty-three-foot-tall air purification system, consuming 1,400 watts of power—no more than a tea kettle—and clean around 30,000 cubic metres of air, each hour meant to clean up parks and other public spaces. The plan is to build the large air purifier and take it on tour around the world to create bubbles of clean air. The machine will harvest smog, which will be compressed into cubes that will be used to make quirky jewellery. Each cube will be made from smog collected from 1,000 cubic metres of poor quality air. Using ion technology, the tower attracts and captures the small pollution particles PM2.5 and PM10 and releases clean air, leaving the surrounding area with air that is about 75 per cent cleaner.

Now, let us look at the second items in the Maslow's hierarchy—the water. Anytime in the history of mankind, fresh water was a precious commodity. Human civilisations have always developed on the sources of water. A constant supply of the same played a significant role in the development of all the ancient civilisations. The first known Greek philosophical thinkers and medical writers also recognised the importance of water for the public health. Alcmaeon of Croton, Hippocrates and Vitruvius, Pliny the Elder, and Galen were the few thinkers and doctors who understood the importance of water for human. Some of the aqueducts that were built for the transport of water played a significant role in the history of engineering. The antique tunnel built by Eupalinus of Megara in 530 BS, to supply water to the

Greek city of Samos, travelled under a mountain ridge for a length of over a kilometre. The construction was done using chisels and hammer, taking around ten years, and serving the city for over 1,000 years. Later, the Romans started to build aqueducts made of covered or open channels, and usually carried over arches supported by tall columns. Water was sourced from mountains through these channels in a slight incline. Romans had the best of such systems to transport fresh water to the households, and to transport dirty water out of the city. Even though there were aqueducts in Rome, none matches the grand monumental double arch portion called Porta Maggiore, which is just the six-mile portion of the giant aqueduct, which is forty-three miles long build by Caligula and Claudius around AD 40. Such aqueducts served the generations and not a few people.

Pollution of such a precious commodity is, again, not a new phenomenon. In fact, pollution has been a problem since the appearance of our earliest ancestors. Increasing human populations have opened the door to more bacteria and diseases. These epidemics were directly related to unsanitary conditions caused by human and animal wastes and garbage. In 1347, the bacterium *Yersinia pestis* carried by rats and spread by fleas, caused the Black Death—an outbreak of bubonic plague. Unsanitary conditions provided the perfect environment for the deadly bacteria to flourish. By the 1800s, people began to understand that unsanitary living conditions and water contamination contributed to disease epidemics. This new awareness prompted major cities to take measures to control waste and garbage. In the mid-1850s, Chicago built the first major sewage system in the United States to treat wastewater.

The start of industrialisation and the related growth of cities created a situation where public health and environmental and water problems overwhelmed city governments to a greater degree. As industrialisation has spread around the globe, the problem of water pollution has spread with it. When earth's population was much smaller, no one believed pollution would ever present a serious problem. It was once popularly believed that the oceans were far too big to pollute. Today, with around seven billion people on the planet, it has become apparent that there are limits. A 1969 United Nations report defined ocean pollution as 'the introduction by man, directly or indirectly, of substances or energy into the marine environment (including estuaries), resulting in such deleterious effects as harm to living resources, hazards to human health, hindrance to marine activities including fishing, impairment of quality for use of sea water, and reduction of amenities'. According to 2013 figures from the World Health Organization, some 780 million people (11 per cent of the world's population) don't have access to safe drinking water, while 2.5 billion (40 per cent of the world's population) don't have proper sanitation (hygienic toilet facilities). Although there have been great improvements in securing access to clean water, relatively little progress has been made on improving global sanitation in the last decade. Sewage disposal affects people's immediate environments and leads to water-related illnesses such as diarrhoea that kills 760,000 children under five each year.

In today's world, over 10,000 people die every day due to diseases like dysentery, cholera, and various diarrhoeal diseases caused by a lack of safe water and adequate sanitation. In India alone, the number of people who die due to water-related illness is around 580. About 90 per cent of the water in the cities of China is polluted. As of 2007, half a billion Chinese had no access to safe drinking water. The most recent national report on water quality in the United States estimates that around 44 per cent of assessed stream miles, 64 per cent of assessed lake acres, and 30 per cent of assessed bays and estuarine square miles were classified as polluted.

The modern contamination is not just by pathogens, it includes the wide spectrum of chemicals too. This results in physical changes of water including temperature and colour. High concentrations of naturally occurring substances or even the manmade chemicals have devastating impacts on aquatic flora and fauna. According to the environmental campaign organization, WWF, 'Pollution from toxic chemicals threatens life on this planet. Every ocean and every continent, from the tropics to the once pristine Polar Regions, is contaminated.'

Surface waters that get polluted with oil spills of ocean and groundwater that get contaminated by the ground drain of harmful chemicals are the two types of water resources that pollution affects. Most water pollution doesn't begin in the water itself. Around 80 per cent of ocean pollution enters our seas from the land. When farmers fertilise the fields, and when chemicals are released by smokestacks and then brought down by rain, groundwater and surface waters are getting affected.

Another source is the electronic waste that is being generated the current era. We use one of the highly toxic chemicals, such as polychlorinated biphenyls (PCBs), non-biodegradable substance, the plastic and heavy metals such as lead, cadmium, and mercury for making our electronic items ranging from computers to mobile phones, automotive parts, and batteries.

It is estimated that around a million tonnes of PCBs were discharged into the environment during the twentieth century. The plastic that we use on our daily life is also a key pollutant of water. Just to give a perspective of the impact that we are making on environment, a plastic bottle can survive an estimated 450 years in the ocean and plastic fishing line can last up to 600 years. In the early 1990s, marine scientist, Tim Benton, collected debris from a 2km (1.5 mile) length of beach in Ducie Atoll, 293 miles away from the nearest inhabited island, Pitcairn Islands in the South Pacific. Along a 1.5-mile stretch of the beach, he counted 953 pieces of garbage, including 6 light bulbs, 171 bottles, a tinned meat pie, 113 buoys, half a toy airplane, 25 shoes, and a plastic foot mat from a car. According to him, fewer than thirty passing yachts stop on the island each year. Just believe the extent of damage that we have done to Mother Earth.

Though there are multiple sources of the pollution, sewage waste is one of the main concerns for the water pollution. As the humanity creeps towards ten billion populations by 2100, it might seem a reasonable question to ask how humanity will deal with this output of feces as the world's population. More than 200 million tonnes of human waste goes untreated every year. In the developing world, 90 per cent of sewage is discharged directly into lakes, rivers, and oceans. Forty per cent of the global population—or 2.5 billion urban residents—practise open defecation or otherwise lack adequate sanitation, and an additional 2.1 billion urban residents use facilities that do not safely dispose of human waste. In India, it is estimated that bad sanitation practises cost the country nearly US$54 billion a year, or 6.4 per cent of its GDP.

Do you really think even if you have a toilet flush, your sewage waste is taken care? No, when you flush the toilet, the waste sinks to the ground and contaminates ground water, else, the sewage waste makes it was untreated into the sea. In theory, sewage is a completely natural substance that should be broken down harmlessly in the environment: 90 per cent of sewage is water. In practise, sewage contains all kinds of other chemicals, from the pharmaceutical drugs people take to the paper, plastic, and other wastes they flush down their toilets.

The next high impact area of water pollution is the nutrient sediments that are rich elements, such as nitrogen and phosphorus, that are washed away as fertilisers from the fields. The sources include the items that we use in our daily lives, such as detergents used in washing machines and dishwashers, pesticides in our garden, chemicals from spilled fuel, broke tyres, brake fluids, etc. These elements with the sewage form a perfect blend for the massive increase in the growth of algae or plankton that overwhelms huge areas of oceans, lakes, or rivers—known as algal bloom. It is harmful because it removes oxygen from the water, which kills other forms of life, leading to what is known as a dead zone. The Gulf of Mexico has one of the world's most spectacular dead zones. According to National Oceanic and Atmospheric Administration, each summer it grows to an area of around 5,500 square miles (14,000 square kilometres), which is slightly smaller than the area of Kuwait. The industrial waste that is expelled every year accumulates to around ten billion ton, which is pumped untreated into rivers, oceans, and other waterways.

Bill and Melinda Gates Foundation has been working on this concern of pollution; employing the techniques of combustion, supercritical water oxidation, and pyrolysis; and has perfected a treatment processes to process fecal sludge—a mixture of human excreta and water. This process is intended to address the large number of existing pit latrines in developing world and support the local. Janicki Bioenergy, a firm working with the foundation, is expecting to convert up to fourteen tonnes of sewage into potable water and electricity each day. If the plant hits the developing world, it is expected to process sewage for a community of about one hundred thousand people. The benefits of the project are enormous.

The promising technology on this area is the nanotechnology. With the modern ultrafiltration techniques and nanotechnology, there are projects and companies such as LIFESAVER Jerrycan, Stellenbosch University Water Institute, HOPE Project, and SlingShot project that are trying to remove such elements in the urban/rural water and make it drinkable. If we could tap the vast oceans as a source of drinking water, everyone would have more than enough. But that means removing the salt, which is inefficient and costly using existing technology. There are works on ceramic and membrane technology to do an efficient filtering of the seawater.

The planet belongs neither to a particular individual nor a particular nation nor it belongs to a specific generation. It belongs not just to humans but to all living creatures, both alive now and in the future. The political and economic institutions of our generation are fixated on enjoying the present, and unable to account for the consequences of our actions on tomorrow. To bear the fruits of what we have been doing since the human inception, we have to be adaptive, and we cannot ignore that. The question is how much we have to adapt either to remain with the tag of the species that is heating the Earth at a rate of two degrees or to graduate to the tag of heating at a rate of four degrees! Have you ever thought what a four-degree average global temperature increase represent?

To give a perspective, oceans cover around 70 per cent of Earth's crust and have the ability to absorb more heat rather than land. This results in land getting more heated approximately by six to twelve degrees in the tropics. If we get to the league of four-degree rise of global temperature, we are talking about a summer temperature of fifty around the tropics. This will seriously affect the infrastructure of any tropical country that was not designed for this four-degree rise of temperature. On the agriculture output, according to WHO, we could expect a 30–40 per cent reduction in the yields of rice and wheat. According to Alice Larkin of Tyndall Centre for Climate Change, we would need to reduce the emissions by 10 per cent. To give a perspective, any control on emissions, more than 1 per cent have always been associated with economic recession according to Nicholas Stern, the leading economist on climate change and chairman of the Grantham Research Institute.

Are we still thinking on how our activities will make us and the future generations pay?

THE AGGLOMERATION THROUGH HYPERLOOP TRANSPORT

A few months back I had been to a prominent hospital since my dad had to undergo an orthopedic surgery. During my stay at the hospital, I got quite accustomed with the staff and they showed me an uncommon transport mechanism. It moves the patient's blood samples and prescription medicines across the hospitals through Pneumatic tubes. They are systems that propel cylindrical containers through networks of tubes by compressed air or by a partial vacuum. Even though it is an age old technology, of the late 19th and 20th century for offices that needed to transport small, urgent packages (such as mail, paperwork, or money) over short distances within a building, or, at most within a city, I was impressed with the precision and the swiftness of the transport. This mode of transportation was invented by William Murdoch in London to transmit telegrams, to nearby buildings from telegraph stations. How do they work?

Assume that a docket has to be moved from department A to department B. The document to be send is enclosed in a large metal packages called the sending station with a door that opens onto a tube. The tube is made of something like PVC plastic or a strong lightweight metal such as aluminum that runs all the way from department A to department B often only a short distance but sometimes up to 600m. These tubes will also have exchanges that are connected with doors that lock with keys or open with numeric keypads and PIN numbers. These exchanges are the connections that connect the department A to department B. At the receiving station, department B the tube connects to a more sophisticated box. This is the powered station, that provides the air power that moves these packages back and forth. It's essentially the same as the sending station, but it has a compressed air pump attached that can either suck air from the tube or blow air into it according to which way down the tube packages need to be sent. Often, the sending and receiving stations have chimes, ringers, or flashing lights to signal when a package has just been received. Typically, canisters are about 5–15cm in diameter and 20–30cm long, made of a toughened plastic such as polycarbonate, and have rubbery bumpers at the ends to provide a good air seal and prevent noise as they travel down the tubes. They unscrew at one end to carry small items weighing up to about 2kg or so at speeds of up to 10m per second or 36 km per hour roughly 5–6 times faster than a person can walk. Can such an integrated system be the framework of our future transport? Can this be the working model of the proposed hyperloop powered by pneumatic energy?

The history of goods transportation closely parallels the history of civilization. The desire to create a viable transportation system to move people and goods is directly related to humanity's eventual transition from a nomadic existence of hunters and gatherers to the sedentary existence of an agrarian society. For the first 2–3 million years of human existence, primitive societies were composed of hunters and gatherers living in what we would today recognize as subsistence. As humans evolved, human power, on foot, was the only method available to transport life necessities to where they were needed. We the homo sapiens have an amazing form of transport build in ourselves. Shanks pony (the human foot!) – one of the main elements of movement of locomotion among the legged animals. The development of inverted pendulum movement around the hip is a landmark development in the history of species evolution. Inspired by the aspiration to travel farther, explore more territory, and expand the influence over larger and larger areas we have gone beyond the usual mode of Shanks pony – the species locomotion to advanced models of transport. As a method of movement through external devices or paraphernalia, land and water were the medium that were identified by our species to commute. Much later came the air as mode of transport. We created first earth tracks to carry goods and they were the precursors to our modern roads. As a matter of fact, these tracks naturally created points of high traffic density. Once the animals were domesticated these tracks couldn't carry the people and the animals that would full fill the trade requirements of our species. This was the key driver for the development of wheel, which happened during the late Neolithic, an era that was much latter than the development of agriculture and of pottery. To give a perspective, potter's wheel was invented around 4000BC, but the spoked wheel and the chariot was invented around 3000BC. The oldest securely dated real wheel-axle combination, that from Stare Gmajne near Ljubljana in Slovenia dated at 3000 BC. Perfecting the art of the cart and the wheel powered by large domesticated animals, such as camels, horses, or oxen was done by the Sumerians sometime around 3000 BC.

It was the Roman who completely made use of the need for good roads to extend and maintain their empire and developed Roman roads. The Romans were the first civilization to develop an identifiable road network to facilitate conquest and movement throughout the growing empire. They were also the first civilization to use a more efficient means of land propulsion in the form of horses on a widespread basis. In this era, larger goods were moved by boat and oar through a network of the known navigable rivers of Europe and Asia. Roman roads were of several kinds, ranging from small local roads to broad, long-distance highways built to connect cities, major towns and military bases. These major roads were often stone-paved and metaled, cambered for drainage, and were flanked by footpaths, bridleways and drainage ditches. They were laid along accurately surveyed courses, and some were cut through hills, or conducted over rivers and ravines on bridgework. Sections could be supported over marshy ground on rafted or piled foundations. At the peak of Roman empire there were 29 military highways that started from the capital, and all the late Empire's 113 provinces were interconnected by 372 great roads. The whole network of interconnected roads of the Roman empire comprised of more than 400,000 kilometres of roads, of which over 80,500 kilometres were stone-paved and maintained. The Romans had the Laws of the Twelve Tables, that specified the dimensions of the road. It shall be 8 Roman feet (around 2.37 m) wide where straight and twice that width where curved. Digital geography expert Raphael Reimman and interactive designer Philipp Schmitt mapped pretty much all roads in Europe and identified that all roads do lead to Rome. The team mapped over 400,000 starting points across the continent and the resulting route from each to Italy's capital, which proves the proverb to the dot. The Roman road network also allowed the development of the cursus publicus, a messenger service that facilitated communications throughout the vast empire, which was the precursor for the modern mail and parcel services.

In fact, early nomadic human tribes did not often need to transport food and water over long distances. Instead, tribes moved along with food and water sources, as humans shifted and settled until water and food needed to be found again. As civilization slowly became agrarian, agricultural settlements were established near fresh water sources like inland rivers or lakes. Water sources served two basic economic needs. Water was an absolute necessity for growing food and sustaining human lives, and offered increasing mobility to expanding sedentary communities. This lead to the evolution of water transport using boats. The ancient boats are supposed to be dugout canoes – boats made from a hallowed tree trunk - developed independently by various stone age civilization and used for coastal fishing and travel. The development of a human civilization dependent upon water sources was complementary with the first major revolution in goods transportation. This was the development of water-borne movement, an activity that appears to predate agrarian society. At the most basic level, a need to catch fish using paddled rafts enabled early societies to hunt for food across a reasonable distance over water. Effective fishing and hunting territory was increased with the development of the sail as a supplement to waterborne travel. They built large merchant ships called cortia, which could carry up to 1,000 tons of cargo. Roman ships had a single main mast, which carried a rectangular sail, although some ships also had small sails at the bow and stern. Roman ships did not have rudders. Instead they were steered by oars. The Romans also built lighthouses to aid shipping.

Egyptians were the first ones even before the Romans to use the concept of building boats from papyrus reeds which were widely cultivated along the Nile River and Delta and tar. Then they started to use various types of wood with ropes and Khufu's solar boat that was made around 2500 B.C. These Egyptian boats were made of either native woods or conifers from Lebanon. Papyrus boats were useful for hunting or crossing short stretches of water, using a paddle or a pole. These boats were made of bundles of bound papyrus reeds, and were lashed together into a long thin hull form in the style of a slight crescent. This lifted the ends out of the water. The bundle was made as wide as possible for stability, and an extra bundle was put on top so that the cargo and crew were kept reasonable dry. This was the beginning of the water transport. Then came the usage of sail harnessing the wind power for locomotion. The best estimates place the invention of the sail at around 2000 BC in Polynesian societies based in Eastern Asia that inhabited around enormous water bodies.

This ignited the need to trade considering the demand and supply of items in individual geographic territory. By developing and exploiting their domestic resources, countries could produce a surplus, and trade this for the resources they need. The evolution of major cities and all permanent human settlement can be traced to the comparative advantage of places with respect to goods trade. This locational advantage is derived from the ease with which goods and people can be transported and traded with respect to other important locations. Advances in goods or freight transportation been always been inspired by a desire for new markets or improved transportation routes between trading nations. A common theme for major improvements in transportation technology have often been driven by military considerations too. Romans not only were pioneers in the land transport. They built large merchant ships, which could carry up to 1,000 tons of cargo. Roman ships had a single main mast, which carried a rectangular sail, although some ships also had small sails at the bow and stern. Roman ships did not have rudders. Instead they were steered by oars. The Romans also built lighthouses to aid shipping. With the decline of the interest in global dominion by the Romans and the subsequent decline of their power, there was a substantial impact on the productivity of transportation. Ultimately, the importance of permanent settlement and the development of land transportation networks waned for the next 1000 years as Western civilization moved into the Dark Ages and the pre-Renaissance era.

With the invention of steam engine, and the introduction of automation of engines through the power of steam into ships, trains and cars in the early 19th century, transformed the logistics industry for ever. Even though there had been variations in the technologies, we still rely on the modified forms of such transport mechanisms through the know medium. But is the future of transport going to be the same in the coming decades? The innovations that are taking the center stage are the driverless cars and public transports and hyper loops. Why they are so important for the human civilization? Let us see why this concept would make sense?

In a nut shell, when I look at the evolving concept of the driving and the driverless cars, they are going to revolutionalise the world for good or for bad.

The greatest impact is on the ownership of the vehicle. People need not own their cars, it will be a service that will be provided by a few companies who own fleets of self-driving vehicles. This will underline the dominance of world's economy and the transport by companies such as Uber, Google and Amazon. So the common man will have to forget the maintenance of the vehicle, insurance to be paid and most probably his/her own dearest "car". The concept of holding a car will get transformed into a pay-as-you-go service. But is it right? Soon we could see a tremendous transfer of wealth to a very small number of people who own the software, battery/power manufacturing, vehicle servicing and charging/power generation/maintenance infrastructure.

With a ball park calculation, every car does approximately 1000 trips a year. This suggests an average of just under 18 trips per car every week. Since the duration of the average car trip is about 20 minutes, the typical car is only on the move for 6 hours in the week: for the remaining 162 hours it is stationary – parked. Since there are 168 hours in a week, the typical car is parked 96.5% of the time. Navigant Research estimates that there are 1.2 Billion Vehicles On World's roads now and assuming a cost of $7000 per vehicle we are talking about 8.4 Trillion dollars. Such a cumulative resource is used less than 5% of time. Now let us look at the parking lots for such vehicles. Eran Ben-Joseph, a Professor and Head of the Department of Urban Studies and Planning at the Massachusetts Institute of Technology has come out with an interesting calculation on the economic efficiency of reducing parking lots. There are an estimated 800 million car parking spaces in the US alone. It amounts to about 3,515 square miles (9,104 sq km). Covering this whole area with solar panels could generate enough electricity to power 11 million households for a month. If we decide to covering only 50% of this area with trees, the drive could remove 1,260,805 tons of carbon dioxide per year. Either way it is a win-win situation. In future, there may not be any parking lots or parking spaces on roads or in buildings. Garages may be re-purposed as mini loading docks for people and deliveries. Aesthetics of homes and commercial buildings will change as parking lots and spaces go away. Surprising part would be that drivers may no longer required and hence the driver's licenses will also slowly go away as with the Department of Motor Vehicles in most countries. This may also result in the traffic policing becoming a redundant job.

When I hear people say that "autonomous cars won't work" I want to ask "Compared to what?". Because human-driven cars don't work very well either. On the economics of self-driving cars, let us analyse the statistics in developed and developing world methodically.

One of the main factors is the most obvious: saved lives and the saved associated economic costs. Globally nearly 1.3 million people die in road crashes each year, on average 3,287 deaths a day. An additional 20-50 million are injured or disabled. Road crashes cost USD $518 billion globally, costing individual countries from 1-2% of their annual GDP. In developing countries such as India, one person dies every 4 minutes in roads accidents in India. This is the statistics revealed by an Indian NGO 'Indians for Road Safety' in 2015. According to World Health Organisation's "Global Road Safety Report-2015" there are 207,551 deaths on roads. The economic cost so estimated for these accidents by International Road Federation amounts to an annual monetary loss of $20 billion. This figure includes expenses associated with the accident victim, property damage and administration expenses. Road crashes cost low and middle-income countries USD $65 billion annually, exceeding the total amount received in developmental assistance.

The story in the developed markets is also not much different. In US alone over 37,000 people die in road crashes each year. Road crashes cost the U.S. $230.6 billion per year, or an average of $820 per person. It may be true that for emotional reasons voters will nevertheless find this unacceptable, but that's no excuse for people rationally discussing costs and benefits to wave away the potential life savings of an autonomous car.

Now let us attach a value to the life saved. The statistical cost of life is an economic value assigned to life in general, or to specific living organisms - it is the marginal cost of death prevention in a certain class of circumstances. The official value for this statistical life used by the Department of Transportation is $9.2 million, so if autonomous cars can save 37,000 lives a year this is a yearly benefit of $340 billion. With an addition of US$ 65 billion low-income and middle-income countries and administration cost of US$ 120 billion, globally, the economic cost of road traffic injuries is about US$ 525 billion a year. I think these reasons justify the efforts.

The second revolution is with the hyperloop. The hybrid of a Concorde and a railgun and an air hockey table – the hyperloop is expected to take the centre stage of this transformation. In a nutshell, the best way to think of the hyperloop is a superfast public transportation that is similar to our Metros. Like the Metro, it would be fast, convenient, cheap, and fairly easy to access. The difference is that instead of taking you from old Delhi to New Delhi in 30-40 minutes, the hyperloop would take you from Delhi to Gwalior (350 kms) in about 20 minutes. Even though it is not an innovative concept, the idea has gained enough of traction. India too plans for its working hyperloop in the coming decade! The first outlay is expected from New Delhi to Mumbai in 70 minutes flat, or three times faster than a commercial flight (a max speed of 760 miles per hour). The pilot funding of expected at $120 million. On the revenue side, a single tube could carry 1.44 lakh passengers daily at 40-second intervals with an average ticket price of under Rs 600 (around 10 dollars).

So how does it work? According to Elon Musk, the pro-pounder of the system, it is a tube over or under the ground that contains a special low-pressure environment. The cars are propelled through this tube with high-speed fans that would compress and push the air for their propulsion. These cars would be floated in the chamber with Air bearings that would make these capsules to levitate in the tube to reduce friction. The entire system will be driven by solar power.

Now let us look at the economics of this transportation system.

The transportation sector as we see it is around 5 trillion dollar industry and for developed countries such as US the industry represents around 8% of the GDP and for developing countries such as India, it represents around 15% of GDP. But what about the public transportation sector? According to the estimates by PWC, Asia-Pacific remains by far the largest transport infrastructure market, with investments increasing from $557bn per year to nearly $900bn per year in 2025. In the next few decades, it will be one of the industries that may see innovations significant number of innovations. It may just not the ones that we have imagined.

Can this technology play a bigger role to play in the future of freight transport too – an industry that powers the global trade? The vision of hyperloop is to connect cities into mega-regions, and turn metro areas into metro stops and thus making a geographical cluster. Given that the technology is planning to move containers and pallets on-demand at speeds far in excess of today's rail and highway options and far less expensively than by air freight, an integrated framework of such seamless nodal transport would be the future of not just human transport but of the goods too. This will reduce the inventory costs and have a better supply chain around each nodal city. Technically this is mentioned in economics as agglomeration – clustering of people and firms. This can lead to more innovative delivery mechanisms of medical/perishable goods and motivate regional economies for greater specialisation, thus reducing the overall cost and quality of global freight transport.

The feasibility of the project has been studies for a specific use case. First full-scale feasibility study into the technology was conducted in evaluating the feasibility of transport between Helsinki, Finland with Stockholm, Sweden. The distance is mere 500 kilometers (311 miles) of Hyperloop track. It takes around 17.5 hours on an overnight ferry or 3.5 hours by air – including the aforementioned security groping and queueing. This distance could be trimmed down to just 28 minutes. On the cost side of it, the estimates project that the 311 miles of track would cost 19 billion euros (about $21 billion at today's rates) to build, which is a lot, but the time savings alone are worth 321 million euros ($355M) per year. Revenue from fares would ring in at a billion euros ($1.1

billion) per year, with an operating profit of 800 million ($885M) based on 43 million passenger trips. If our grossly oversimplified math is right, that'd put the fare price at just under $26. The addition of freight transport would likely speed up the money-making process even further.

But what makes Hyperloop One's study truly fascinating is how it shapes up to high-speed rail projects. An Hyperloop connection between the Scandinavian capitals would cost just 38 million euros ($42 million) per kilometer, compared to 100M euros ($110M) per kilometer for the high-speed rail line between the British cities of London and Birmingham. And the new train project in California? That's going for $76.4 to $87.4 million per kilometer. Although this was a study done by Hyperloop, World bank also did a similar study. On a global scale the cost per-mile for building this loop is pegged at around $40 million per kilometre compared to High-Speed rail project at $56 million per km. In any way this is one of the best transport mechanism in today's prices.

This technology is not without risks. According to Dr. Phil Mason from Cornell University, any failure whatsoever will rip the outer tube like candy. Anybody in the capsule would die pretty much instantly in the event of a crash...but a single breach in the Hyperloop would probably kill everybody else in the Hyperloop because air would rush into the tube at about the speed of sound. On the practicality of the project, for the Hyperloop to work, it would need a way to pump out roughly 2 million cubic meters of air from its tubes and make sure that the air stays out of a 373 mile-long pipe with walls less than an inch thick. Intolerable heat and the Terrorist activities are another set of problems that hyperloop would face.

Despite all these, the hyperloop hype is rationalised by it low cost. A trip on it expected to cost around $20, or about the cost of a bus ticket, yet it would be faster and more convenient than airliners or a car. Like the automobile and the train before it, such a system would change our society and economy beyond recognition. This technology could drive most airlines out of business. Nobody would bother to fly if the hyperloop was available for travel between most destinations inside the American and European continent. It would be cheaper, faster, and more convenient, even for transcontinental travel. Air travel could be restricted to transoceanic flights and hobbyists or rich people. This could impact the discount airlines, since one could simply walk or take the bus over to a station, and get on the hyperloop, and make the same trip in a similar or faster time frame.

The funniest problem would be the of abandoned airports. Similar to that of abandoned train stations a generation ago, or that of empty malls today most airports could end up being abandoned because the business would disappear. It is possible that a few large regional airports might remain for intercontinental travel, but most airports would eventually shut down. Airports in large urban areas could simply be redeveloped, while ones in many smaller cities could simply be abandoned. Housing costs could be under pressure since people could live farther and commute over long distances. This could ease out the prices in our expensive cities such as Mumbai and Delhi, where there are currently shortages that lead to high priced housing. We could expect an economic boom in areas with lots of cheap housing that is in fairly close proximity to expensive urban areas since the dwellers could have additional disposable income to spend rather than rent.

But where would people concentrate? As usual where the government has lower tax structure. People could folk to areas that have lower tax and thus make more disposable income. The car ownership will be reduced with this concept since the commuting will be much more efficient and the ownership of the car will be reduced. Many people would simply ditch the car if they could get to whatever recreational activity they enjoy in 30 minutes. Result would be an increase the demand for ride-sharing services like Uber and short term car rental services.

The railroads may get their track converted into hyperloops rights away. With the hyperloops and the self-driving trucks in place, long haul trucking industry would go for a logistics revolution by providing a cheaper and more efficient means of shipping goods. This would result in the reducing the cost of many goods by greatly reducing transportation costs. Oil and gas is one industry that could see a heavy impact. The demand for oil would reduce because the hyperloop would run on electricity and that too powered by solar panels.

The bottom line is that Hyperloop could transform the world into a different place with a very different economy and different habits. Those kinds of changes would transform our lives profoundly. The hyperloop could be the ultimate disruptive technology and change our society beyond recognition. If the hyperloop works, world could be a place of empty freeways, abandoned airports, and vast junkyards full of cars, and airliners waiting for the scrapheap. Elon Musk could be remembered like Henry Ford, James Watt, and Thomas Edison, a man who transformed the world beyond recognition with his technology.

www.ingramcontent.com/pod-product-compliance
Lightning Source LLC
Chambersburg PA
CBHW051648170526
45167CB00001B/384